Destination Collaboration 2

DESTINATION COLLABORATION 2

A Complete Reference Focused Curriculum Guidebook to Educate 21st Century Learners in Grades 3–5

Danielle N. DuPuis and Lori M. Carter

 LIBRARIES UNLIMITED

AN IMPRINT OF ABC-CLIO, LLC

Santa Barbara, California • Denver, Colorado • Oxford, England

Library of Congress Cataloging-in-Publication Data

DuPuis, Danielle N.
    Destination collaboration 2 : a complete reference focused curriculum guidebook to educate 21st century learners in grades 3-5 / Danielle N. DuPuis and Lori M. Carter.
        p. cm.
    Includes bibliographical references and index.
    ISBN 978-1-59884-583-9 (acid-free paper) — ISBN 978-1-59884-584-6 (ebook)   1. Information literacy—Study and teaching (Elementary)   2. Electronic information literacy—Study and teaching (Elementary)   3. School librarian participation in curriculum planning.   4. Library orientation for school children.   5. Reference books.
I. Carter, Lori M.   II. Title.
    ZA3075.D872 2011
    372.13'0281—dc22   2010035226

ISBN: 978-1-59884-583-9
EISBN: 978-1-59884-584-6

15   14   13   12   11   1   2   3   4   5

This book is also available on the World Wide Web as an eBook.
Visit www.abc-clio.com for details.

Libraries Unlimited
An Imprint of ABC-CLIO, LLC

ABC-CLIO, LLC
130 Cremona Drive, P.O. Box 1911
Santa Barbara, California 93116-1911

This book is printed on acid-free paper ∞

Manufactured in the United States of America

Standards for the 21st-Century Learner by the American Association of School Librarians, a division of the American Library Association, copyright © 2007 American Library Association. Available for download at www.ala.org/aasl/standards. Used with permission.

NETS for Students: National Educational Technology Standards for Students, Second Edition, © 2007, ISTE ® (International Society for Technology in Education), www.iste.org. All rights reserved.

Standards for the English Language Arts, by the International Reading Association and the National Council of Teachers of English, Copyright 1996 by the International Reading Association and the National Council of Teachers of English. Reprinted with permission.

National Standards for History, Revised Edition (UCLA: 1996), available: http://nchs.ucla.edu. Used with permission.

National Science Education Standards reprinted with permission from *National Science Education Standards, 1996* by the National Academy of Sciences, Courtesy of the National Academy Press, Washington, D.C.

National Social Studies Standards © National Council for the Social Studies. Reprinted by permission.

Contents

3RD-GRADE LESSONS
Lesson 1: Encyclopedia 101

Lesson 2: Encyclopedia Trivia

4TH-GRADE LESSONS

Lesson 1: Information Station

Lesson 2: Encyclopedia Retail

5TH-GRADE LESSONS

Lesson 1: Encyclopedia Disaster

Lesson 2: Newsworthy Events

3RD-GRADE LESSONS

Lesson 1: Around the World

Lesson 2: A-T-L-A-S

4TH-GRADE LESSONS
Lesson 1: Getting to Know the World

Lesson 2: Planning a Trip

5TH-GRADE LESSONS

Lesson 1: Postcards from Pedro

Lesson 2: Location Nation

Lesson 2: Did You Know?

4TH-GRADE LESSONS

Lesson 1: Magazine Mania!

Lesson 2: Start the Presses

5TH-GRADE LESSONS

Lesson 1: Time Stands Still

Lesson 2: Off to the Future

3RD-GRADE LESSONS

Lesson 1: Who's Who in Our Class

Lesson 2: Classmate Biographies

4TH-GRADE LESSONS
Lesson 1: Famous American Biographies

Lesson 2: Name of the Game

5TH-GRADE LESSONS

Lesson 1: Biography Résumé

Lesson 2: Getting a Job

Acknowledgments

We would like to thank Shellie Elson from National Council of Teachers of English (NCTE), Chi Yang from National Council for the Social Studies (NCSS), Barbara Murphy from National Academies Press, Marian Olivas from National Center for History in the Schools, Tina Wells from International Society for Technology in Education (ISTE), and Alison Cline from American Association of School Librarians (AASL). Thank you so much for taking the time to communicate with us and for giving us permission to use the national standards in our books.

The lessons in this book were created by following the backward design model. Thank you to Grant Wiggins and Jay McTighe for writing *Understanding by Design* to better explain this process.

A big thank you goes out to our teacher and colleague Dr. Ann Weeks. Thank you for encouraging us to write this book, and for your support along the way.

We'd also like to thank Sharon Coatney, our editor and guiding light during the last year of our three-year journey in writing the *Destination Collaboration* books. We really appreciate your guidance and support!

Our acknowledgments wouldn't be complete without mentioning and thanking our families, who have "put up" with us these last few years as we worked evenings and weekends on *Destination Collaboration*.

Danielle dedicates this book in loving memory of her grandfather, who continues to serve as her inspiration.

Lori dedicates this book in loving memory of her father, who always "believed in doing it 'till you get it right," and her mother, who still provides much love and support. She also dedicates this book to her husband, Rick Carter, with much love for his constant support. And to their children, Lindsey, Kelley, Chelsea, Rita, Jason, and Brianna: thank you for understanding the amount of effort involved in writing a book.

Permissions

As with any valuable educational resource, it is of great assistance to other educators to see how the standards are applied for use in student instruction. The various national standards reprinted in this book have been done so within the guidelines of permissible use as associated with each organization. Following is a list of the each organization with a link to each organizations Web site. Use these Web sites as a resource when creating your own collaborative cross-curricular lesson plans.

Excerpted from *Standards for the 21st-Century Learner* by the American Association of School Librarians, a division of the American Library Association, copyright © 2007 American Library Association. Available for download at www.ala.org/aasl/standards. Used with permission.

Curriculum Standards for Social Studies © National Council for the Social Studies. Reprinted by permission. http://www.socialstudies.org/.

Standards for the English Language Arts, by the International Reading Association and the National Council of Teachers of English, Copyright 1996 by the International Reading Association and the National Council of Teachers of English. Reprinted with permission. http://www.ncte.org/standards.

National Educational Technology Standards for Students, Second Edition, © 2007, ISTE® (International Society for Technology in Education), Reprinted with permission. www.iste.org All rights reserved.

National Science Education Standards Reprinted with permission from the National Science Education Standards, 2008 by the National Academy of Sciences, Courtesy of the National Academies Press, Washington, D.C.

National Standards for History, "National Standards for History, revised edition" (UCLA: 1996). Reprinted with permission. http://nchs.ucla.edu.

Introduction

Destination Collaboration 2: A Complete Reference Focused Curriculum Guidebook to Educate 21st Century Learners in Grades 3–5 is designed to assist library media specialists and classroom teachers in creating instructional partnerships. This book includes four chapters with comprehensive instructional units for grades 3, 4, and 5—totaling 24 original lesson plans. Each unit is rooted in classroom content and focuses on: using library resources, incorporating information literacy skills, and using technology to deliver meaningful and memorable instruction to students. Each chapter in this book contains two lesson plans for each grade level on a particular media unit: encyclopedias, atlases, almanacs, and biographies. These units were chosen as the basis for each chapter, because elementary students must become familiar with each basic reference tool in order to be successful at solving inquiry problems.

This book is not meant to be read in one sitting or from cover to cover. Instead, we hope that you will use the lessons as needed to cover relevant information literacy topics and content area objectives with your students. The lessons in this book are designed with the assumption that you are *not* fully collaborating with every teacher in your building *all* the time. Each lesson is designed knowing that the possibility exists that you may teach this lesson in isolation, coordination, cooperation, or collaboration. In addition, we also offer the ability to use the lesson topic in an inquiry-based format. These premade lessons and materials can serve as the building blocks for collaborating with other teachers at your school. Our book not only provides complete lessons, technology options, modifications, student project templates, and inquiry-based learning options, but it also supports your efforts in moving from isolation to coordination and cooperation, and on toward collaboration.

Being Seen as a Leader

The journey toward collaboration requires the use of leadership skills, content knowledge, and information literacy knowledge, along with patience and innovation. Collaboration is most easily implemented when others in the school see you as an instructional leader. Most library media centers are centrally located within a school. We believe the library media center is the "hub" of the school and that library media specialists are in a position where much of the action takes place. We realize that there are many influences that will affect your ability to be a leader in your school: your relationship with administration, your involvement in school improvement meetings, your material selection and evaluation, and the design of your physical space, to name a few. This book is designed to help you be seen as an instructional leader because regardless of what kind of program you find yourself working with today, this book provides the tools and inspiration to move your program toward collaboration.

Information Power (American Association of School Librarians [AASL], 1998) talks about the themes of collaboration, leadership, and technology, but as Keith Curry Lance pointed out, "the three themes [are listed] in the wrong order. Leadership comes first, then collaboration, and then technology. If you want to collaborate, you have to step into those leadership shoes first and establish yourself as a leader that somebody would want to collaborate with" (Achterman, 2007, p. 51).

Collaboration comes when you are seen as an instructional leader. Leadership builds from mutual respect and trust. An instructional leader possesses the ability to design lesson plans, make connections to classroom learning, infuse lessons with technology, include assessment strategies, provide students with modifications and extensions, and have the desire to develop inquiry-based learning units with classroom teachers. This book demonstrates and assists you in putting into practice the aforementioned qualities of an instructional leader.

From Isolation to Collaboration

Effective library media specialists invest a significant amount of time juggling their many duties and jobs. We hope that the materials in this book will help move your relationship with teachers to a higher level: from isolation to coordination, cooperation, or collaboration (ICCC). Each lesson has been designed to enable easy implementation. The introduction in each chapter focuses on the importance of the key topic in that chapter. Relevancy and the importance of the topic are explained. Assessment choices are also discussed.

The circular ICCC indicators seen throughout the book will be repeated in each chapter so that you can easily locate how to share the lessons regardless of your location on the ICCC continuum. Information regarding the use of the lessons in isolation can be found at the beginning of each chapter. These tips are located at the beginning of the chapter because isolation tips provide an overview of why the skill covered in the chapter is important, how it can be incorporated in the classroom, and simple ways to improve visibility within the school. Coordination and cooperation tips are located at the beginning of each individual lesson within the unit. These tips are placed close to the lessons because in order to coordinate and cooperate, your efforts must be connected to your instruction and that of the classroom teacher. Suggestions for collaboration can always be found at the end of each grade-level unit. Collaboration tips are placed at the end of the unit because these tips include essential questions that are directly tied to classroom content. Use these essential questions to create inquiry-based learning projects with classroom teachers.

ICCC Continuum

"Not a single state reading assessment used for No Child Left Behind (U.S. Department of Education, 2007) assessments measures our students' ability to read search engine results; locate information online; critically evaluate information on the Internet; or synthesize information online. It is the cruelest irony of No Child Left Behind Act that students who most need to be prepared at school for an online age of information are precisely those who are being prepared the least" (Leu, O'Byrne, Zawilinski, McVerry, and Everett-Cacopardo, 2009, p. 267).

With the implementation of the No Child Left Behind Act in 2002, the importance of moving toward collaboration is clear. Research has shown that improved student learning occurs when learning goals can be unified across many areas of the curriculum. However, in many schools, library media specialists are still working in isolation for a number of reasons. Teaching in isolation is delivering instruction of one subject to one set of students during one time period. Isolation can be a common byproduct of a fixed schedule in a library media center. As a result, library media specialists' fixed schedules allow for very little flexibility for co-teaching opportunities. Classroom teachers may find it difficult to collaborate. There also may not be enough time in the school day to do more than: teach classes, troubleshoot technology problems, spend your annual budget, weed your collection, and provide professional development. Taking these factors into account, it is easy to understand how even the most effective library media specialists can find moving toward collaboration complicated. By providing you with proper documentation and complete lesson plans, we hope to alleviate some of the pressure of the demands you face. These lessons will help demonstrate your abilities as a teacher. Recognition as a teacher is an important first step as you move away from isolation. This book lessens the amount of time needed to prepare effective lessons as you move around the ICCC continuum (Austin, 2000) with other teachers.

One way to work toward collaboration is to coordinate a lesson or unit with another teacher. Working in coordination is the process of arranging schedules, activities, or resources with another teacher in order to help your own work run more efficiently. The event, project, or activity is coordinated by one person and communicated to someone else. For example, you may be getting ready to start a geography unit with your 4th-grade students that focuses on different cultures around the world. To coordinate a global geography lesson with the classroom teacher, you might ask the classroom teacher when he or she might be teaching global culture. The classroom teacher may ask you to provide him or her with resources that are in your media center. You may also wish to share some materials that you use to teach geography concepts and skills to students. Perhaps the classroom teacher will arrange for you to keep the students for a few extra minutes if you need more time to complete the lessons. If you find yourself in coordination, each lesson in this book provides you with specific examples for how to move from coordination towards cooperation and collaboration.

Cooperation

Cooperation is sometimes mistaken for collaboration; however, they are not the same. The process of cooperation includes setting goals, and working with one or more classroom teachers to share responsibility for creating a project, but the parts of the project may be taught separately. One partner in the team may be assigned a major role while others may take on more limited responsibilities. For example, if you were teaching a unit about the planets with your 3rd-grade students, you might have a lesson plan that has a large research piece as well as a writing piece. The lesson is mostly planned, but you think that it will be beneficial to cooperate with the classroom teacher, so you meet with the classroom teacher to talk about sharing the work. You offer to teach the research piece, and the classroom teacher takes responsibility for the writing assignment. The research piece may take several sessions in the media center to gather all necessary information to write a comprehensive paragraph for the project. Upon completion of the research, the classroom teacher assists the students by teaching proper grammar and sentence structure, and by giving instruction on how to write a research paper. Cooperation does *not* require shared power. Cooperation can begin a partnership by building mutual respect and trust. Each chapter in this book provides suggestions on how to build on that trust as you move towards collaboration with classroom teachers.

Collaboration

When you work together with other teachers and equally contribute to creating and designing integrated instruction, you are working in collaboration. Sharing the planning, design, and implementation of content and media objectives with other teachers should result in new understandings and experiences for both the teacher and the library media specialist. With a shared vision you will work together through an equal partnership to integrate content and information literacy standards to accomplish objectives. To assist you in reaching collaboration, a number of planning documents and handouts have been included in this book. The companion Web site contains electronic worksheets to assist you in asking the right questions as you meet and plan with your instructional partner to create a collaborative lesson or unit. Not only are you provided suggestions for approaching classroom teachers, but we've also included essential questions to assist you in creating inquiry-based research projects and templates for creating your own lessons. These documents may be used to initiate conversation with your instructional partner, as well as to build on and improve the lessons provided in this book.

National Standards

Students are more likely to succeed when cross-curricular connections can be made. The lessons in each chapter support not only the new American Association of School Librarians (AASL) *Standards for the 21st-Century Learner* and current National Educational Technology Standards for Students (NETS-S) technology standards, but they also apply national content area standards including science, social studies, history, and language arts. These content areas were chosen because information literacy skills can be taught effectively through these subject areas and because they offer excellent opportunities to collaborate with the classroom teacher (Corey, 2002).

In the process of writing the lessons in this book, the *Standards for the 21st-Century Learner in Action* (AASL, 2009) were explicitly embedded within each of the lessons to show how the content and structure of the lesson supported the AASL strands and benchmarks. Every applicable indicator for skills, dispositions in action, responsibilities, and self-assessment strategies were embedded within each lesson to create clear connections. We have been granted permission from AASL to indicate the standard number at the beginning of each lesson to show what general AASL standards the lesson addresses. However, the embedded numbered strands and descriptions of the skills, dispositions in action, responsibilities, and self-assessment strategies have been removed so as to comply with copyright. Although these indicators and benchmarks have been removed, embedded placeholders remain for your reference. We strongly encourage the use of the *Standards for the 21st-Century Learner in Action* (AASL, 2009) as a guide to locate the indicators and benchmarks for each skill, disposition in action, responsibility, and self-assessment strategy. We suggest writing the indicators directly onto the embedded placeholders in this book. We realize that going back to look at the standards will take a considerable amount of work and effort; however, going through the motion of looking up the indicators and benchmarks will not only assist you in better understanding how to use the lessons in this book, but it will also provide you with the background knowledge and support needed to create your own lesson plans with embedded standards. As you work to embed the skill indicators, be sure to note that the skill indicators will directly correspond with a specific standard (i.e., Standard 1, 2, 3, or 4). However, the dispositions in action indicators, responsibility indicators, and self-assessment strategy indicators, are all fluid. These indicators may be mixed and matched to support any of the four standards. Be sure to note that these indicators do not necessarily follow the general standard for the lesson. Locating these direct connections will assist you as you rework and create lessons that integrate the use of these new standards. Please refer to the *Standards for the 21st-Century Learner in Action* (AASL, 2009) for more information and integrate the full standards directly into each lesson using the template provided.

Using Technology

We understand the need for the ethical use of information and that "information skills will enable students to use technology as an important tool for learning now and in the future" (AASL, 2007, p. 2). As you explore and use the lessons within this book, you will notice that technology is integrated in most of the lessons through various common applications, Web sites, and suggested use of online databases. If technology is not integrated directly into the lesson, technology options are always included and can be used for lesson extensions, activities, or tools for locating more information. These technology options are located at the end of each lesson and are called either "Technology Integration" or an "Enrichment Using Technology." The "Technology Integration" can be used directly within the lesson as it was written. If you decide to use the "Technology Integration" option, the technology standards have also been included. The options provided in the "Enrichment Using Technology" sections could change the focus of the lesson. Depending on your comfort level with technology, build on the lesson by using the suggested podcasts, blogs, or other Web 2.0 tools. As you use this book, you may wish to add other ideas and technology resources to enhance your lessons. Using these technology suggestions may provide you with a springboard for another collaborative opportunity. You may wish to think about how the purpose of the lesson may change by making these alterations.

Materials

Each lesson includes a number of ready-made materials you may use to assist your students in the learning process. These materials will be found either within the book or on our companion Web site. You may access this Web site at **www.destinationcollaboration. com**. You will notice that we include a variety of materials that appeal to kinesthetic, visual, and auditory learners. Each unit includes a blend of electronic materials such as Power-Point presentations, videos, and electronic worksheets. The PowerPoint presentations in our book are instructional tools and include helpful notes to guide you through instruction, interactive games, and digital photographs. These interactive resources will engage and interest your students in learning information literacy skills and will be found on the companion Web site. In addition, sidebars have been placed within the book to highlight discussion opportunities, 21st century skills, building your own resource, and classroom connections.

How to Read the Labels for Instructional Materials

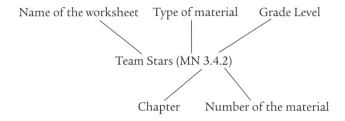

There are several different codes for material types:

MN = Manipulatives are hands-on activities for your students. You may wish to laminate these items and use them from year to year.

WS = Worksheets are for student use and are meant to be printed and photocopied.

EWS = Electronic worksheets are for student use and are meant to be used on a computer or in a computer lab setting. These worksheets can be downloaded from our companion Web site to your computer at any time. We recommend downloading them prior to the lesson for easy access.

RS = Resource sheets are for student use and are meant to provide them with additional or background information.

ER = Electronic resources are electronic teaching tools and are sometimes interactive.

TRS = Teacher resource sheets are for teachers only and provide background information and answers to student resource sheets and worksheets.

MOD = Modified worksheets or resource sheets are provided to assist those students with special developmental or academic needs. You may wish to modify these sheets even further.

EX = Extension activities are sometimes provided to enhance the lesson with an additional activity or worksheet (print or electronic). You can also use these activities for gifted students or early finishers.

O = An "O" at the beginning of any of the aforementioned material codes indicates that the material will be found on our online companion Web site.

Collaborative Documents

The intended use for our book is to provide lesson plans that can be used on an ICCC continuum. In many schools, elementary library media specialists see students on a fixed schedule once a week. As a result, it is very difficult for library media specialists to create inquiry-based learning projects and maintain the cognitive continuity needed for this level of learning by students in just 30 minutes to an hour once a week. Our book includes suggestions for inquiry-based learning projects, which you may wish to use with students. We hope that you will review these lessons and adapt them to meet your needs as well as the needs of your students. This book is designed to support you in your efforts to move toward collaboration with classroom teachers and to improve learning and teaching opportunities within your school.

Inquiry-based learning has been shown to support student achievement. Because of its value, we have included appendices A and B for you to use as you collaborate with classroom teachers to create inquiry-based learning or collaborative lesson plans.

Inquiry-based learning experiences focus on students' own questions about a topic; in this way, student curiosity becomes a driving force for learning. Through such experiences, students locate information, organize it, and share that information with an audience through a variety of forms including writing, multimedia presentations, debates, or Web sites (Moss, 2005).

We hope the examples in appendices A and B will encourage you to work collaboratively with classroom teachers in your building to create integrated learning opportunities. While we know that this book will not be your only lesson planning resource, we hope that it will offer some new ideas and approaches that will enable you to work more effectively with teachers and expand the learning opportunities for your students.

Benefits of Using This Book

"We have to stand by the need for teacher-librarians to be qualified as both teachers and librarians, because if they're not, they're not going to be allowed to do what we want them to do. One thing I'm pretty sure of is that if you're in a public school and you want a teacher to collaborate with you, they'd better perceive you as a teacher or it's just not going to happen" (Achterman, 2007).

Library media specialists are a diverse group. Some of us have experience working as classroom teachers, and others may have experience working in public or private libraries prior to beginning work in the preK–12 environment. No matter what our backgrounds, we do share the same goals as our colleagues in the education field—we promote and teach information literacy, ground our instruction in national standards, encourage and integrate the use of technology, encourage a love of reading, and want our students to succeed at whatever career path they choose. This book will help you be recognized by other educators in the building as a teacher, librarian, information specialist, and instructional partner—commonly known as a library media specialist. It will assist changing perceptions about librarians as "just storytellers" or the "sweet lady/gentleman who only knows how to find and recommend books." Library media specialists are men and women from all walks of life who devote themselves to being lifelong learners and educators. We not only answer questions but also teach students and individuals how to find the answers and why the resources used are important. You are a learner, a leader, program administrator, instructional partner, information specialist, and teacher. In providing you with the necessary tools to teach a unit from start to finish, we hope that this book will encourage and enable you to look at your lessons in a new way and give you an opportunity to be recognized as a 21st century library media specialist.

Works Cited

Achterman, Doug. "The Sower: Interview with Keith Curry Lance." *School Library Journal* 53.10 (2007): 50–53. Print.

American Association of School Librarians. *Information Power: Building Partnerships For Learning.* Chicago: American Library Association, 1998. Print.

American Association of School Librarians. *Standards for the 21st-Century Learner.* Chicago: American Library Association, 2007. American Library Association. Web. 9 Mar. 2008 <http://www.ala.org/ala/mgrps/divs/aasl/guidelinesandstandards/learningstandards/standards.cfm>.

American Association of School Librarians. *Standards for the 21st-Century Learner in Action.* Chicago: American Library Association, 2009. Print.

Austin, James E. *The Collaboration Challenge: How Nonprofits and Businesses Succeed through Strategic Alliances.* San Francisco: Jossey-Bass, 2000. Print.

Corey, Linda. "The Role of the Library Media Specialist in Standards-Based Learning." *Knowledge Quest* (2002): 21–23. *Library Literature and Information Science Full Text.* Web. 12 Nov. 2007.

Leu, Donald J. "New Literacies, Reading Research, and the Challenges of Change: A Deictic Perspective." *The 55th Yearbook of the National Reading Conference.* Milwaukee, WI. 30 Nov. 2005.

Leu, Donald J., Rosemarie Ataya, and Julie L. Coiro. *Assessing Assessment Strategies Among the 50 States: Evaluating the Literacies of Our Past or Our Future?* Paper Presented at the National Reading Conference, Miami, FL, Dec. 2002.

Leu, Donald J., W. Ian O'Byrne, Lisa Zawilinski, J. Greg McVerry, and Heidi Everett-Cacopardo. "Expanding the New Literacies Conversation." *Educational Researcher* 38.4.1 (2009): 264–269. Web. 30 Sept. 2010.

Moss, Barbara. "Making a Case and a Place For Effective Content Area Literacy Instruction in the Elementary Grades." *The Reading Teacher* 59.1 (2005): 46–55. *Library Literature and Information Science Full Text.* Web. 13 Nov. 2007.

U.S. Department of Education. *No Child Left Behind Act of 2001. United States Department of Education.* Web. 15 Nov. 2007 <http://www.ed.gov/policy/elsec/leg/esea02/index.html>.

Works Consulted

Fine, J. "Hand in Hand: Public and School Library Cooperative Projects." *Journal of Youth Services* 14.3 (2001): 18–22. Print.

Hartzell, Gary N. *Building Influence for the School Librarian: Tenet, Targets and Tactics.* 2nd ed. Worthington: Linworth, 2003. Print.

Loertscher, D. V. "Second Revolution: A Taxonomy for the 1980's." *Wilson Library Bulletin* 56 (1982): 412–21. Print.

Loertscher, D. V. *Taxonomies of the School Library Media Program.* Englewood, CO: Libraries Unlimited, 1988. Print.

Loertscher, D. V. *Taxonomies of the School Library Media Program.* 1988. 2nd ed. San Jose, CA: Hi Willow, 2000. Print.

McKenna, M.C., and R.D. Robinson. "Content Literacy: A Definition and Implications." *Journal of Reading* 34 (1990): 184–86. Print.

Montiel-Overall, Patricia. "Toward a Theory of Collaboration for Teachers and Librarians." *School Library Media Research* 8 (2005). *American Association of School Librarians.* Web. 1 Sept. 2007.

Wiggins, Grant, and Jay McTighe. *Understanding By Design*. Alexandria, VA: Association for Supervision and Curriculum Development, 2005. Print.

Chapter 1

Encyclopedias: Using Reference Tools

Introduction

The encyclopedia is a tool students should learn how to use in order to find general information on a wide variety of subjects. An encyclopedia is a natural first stop for beginning research on any topic. Encyclopedias have traditionally been in print only. However, this chapter introduces students to both print and online encyclopedias including Wikipedia—the first formal reference option that has the ability to be rewritten by anyone on the Internet. Through learning how to use and understand the differences between print, online, and Web 2.0 encyclopedias, students will become more information literate.

From Year to Year

The encyclopedia is a reference tool that requires some background knowledge in regards to structure and content in order for basic library users to find what they are looking for. Even when a student understands how to search for information using an encyclopedia, the vocabulary in an encyclopedia may be difficult for the student to comprehend. Building upon the understandings from the previous year, the lessons in this chapter are designed to assist students in becoming proficient library users. The 3rd-grade lessons begin with the basics of performing a simple search using print encyclopedias; students will become familiar with the layout and text features that are commonly used in encyclopedias. In the 4th-grade lessons, students shift from print to online encyclopedias and compare the differences. The lessons for 5th grade are designed to teach students about source reliability and accuracy and require students to use both online encyclopedias and Wikipedia to cross-reference the information through book resources. By gradually introducing these reference tools, students will be better prepared for searching, gathering, and using information in the 21st century.

Lifelong Library Use

The world of information is constantly changing and is widely available to students. As digital natives, students access the Internet as a first choice for finding information. However, students may be unaware the general public has access to publish and alter Web content and may be exposed to unreliable information. Students also have access to reliable and accurate resources. Students need to learn how to utilize reference sources such as encyclopedias to follow up on information that may be misleading or biased. Questioning the reliability and accuracy of information and then using available resources to reinforce or confirm information is a skill that will enable students to be more prepared to handle information appropriately in the future. This type of behavior will encourage independent information seeking strategies among students, thereby creating lifelong library users.

Self-Assessment Strategies

Self-assessments are provided in each grade level unit of this chapter. It is imperative for students to question the validity of resources as well as determine what new understandings may have been acquired and how these new understandings can be applied in other situations or projects. Self-assessment causes students to reflect upon their work and their understandings. Encyclopedias are commonly used to gain background information. The self-assessments included in this chapter prompt students to reflect on the encyclopedia as a reference tool (how it assisted them in answering some, but perhaps not all, questions they had), and for the questions not answered in the encyclopedia, what other types of references are available to them. In these self-assessments, students must also evaluate the effectiveness of the learning product. Being able to independently explore and select appropriate reference tools and information is a skill that will take much-guided practice. By consistently assessing the learning process and learning products, the student will be well on the way to becoming an independent learner and library user.

Relevancy

Collaborative resources, such as Wikipedia, in which anyone can change and edit information, are becoming more prevalent. Now, more than ever, students need to be educated in regards to source content, reliability, relevancy, and accessibility. Scholarly texts, including encyclopedias, will provide students with the relevant and accurate information needed to satisfy their curiosity regarding a number of subjects and topics. The successful navigation of both print and electronic encyclopedias are essential as students gain basic research skills to probe deeper into the strategies of seeking accurate information.

Working in Isolation

Isolation

Knowing how to use the encyclopedia is a skill that students need in order to find general information quickly. Print encyclopedias are still valid and reliable resources, but with the integration of technology, online encyclopedias are cost effective, are easier for students to access, provide a wider range of information, and are updated more frequently. Your students will benefit from learning how a print encyclopedia is structured and how to use text feature skills before moving on to an online encyclopedia. Online encyclopedias offer information that is hyperlinked, and they often include multimedia options such as audio and video. Hyperlinked information gives students another dimension to consider when thinking about how to find information. Be sure that students understand how to use print encyclopedias, and then expand their knowledge to include how to navigate the dynamics of a variety of online encyclopedias. Share Wikipedia with students explaining that as a wiki, this site can be altered by anyone at anytime. Encourage students to double-check facts that they find in Wikipedia.

Take notice when students have a special interest in a particular topic. They may be surprised to learn that they can find information in the encyclopedia about a wide variety of topics. Think about ordering encyclopedias on specific classroom content or students' favorite topics like: dinosaurs, insects, sports, pets, the Civil War, or Native Americans.

Classroom teachers may assign favorite projects each year. Be mindful of this when planning lessons to teach each quarter. Taking note of these special projects and when they occur will provide a great discussion opportunity with the classroom teacher prior to the project being assigned. Also think about the projects classroom teachers are assigning and develop the school's library collection to better serve their needs.

3RD-GRADE LESSONS

LESSON 1: ENCYCLOPEDIA 101

Coordinate! This encyclopedia lesson will introduce students to when, why, and how they should use encyclopedias to satisfy a need for general information. After thinking about something they'd like to learn more about, students use print encyclopedias to locate information to satisfy their own curiosities. *Coordinate* with the classroom teacher by offering the media center's set of encyclopedias to use with students in the classroom for an upcoming project.

Cooperate! Once students have completed this lesson and have filled out the "A Closer Look" (WS 1.3.1) worksheet, share the completed worksheets with the classroom teacher. The classroom teacher will be eager to know what students want to learn more about. *Cooperate* by offering to select some resources that compliment the class' interests for students to check out from the media center, or for the classroom teacher to use to support student interests in the classroom.

Lesson Plan

Integrated Goals:

Language Arts

Standard 8. Students use a variety of technological and information resources (e.g., libraries, databases, computer networks, video) to gather and synthesize information and to create and communicate knowledge.

Library Media

AASL 21st Century Standards

> **Standard 1:** Inquire, think critically, and gain knowledge.
> **Standard 4:** Pursue personal and aesthetic growth.

Essential Questions:

> How can encyclopedias help you answer basic information questions?
> How can text features help you find information in an encyclopedia?

Desired Understandings:

Students will understand:

> How to locate information in an encyclopedia to answer general information questions.
> How to use text features when searching for information in an encyclopedia.

Integrated Objectives:

- Students will learn how to use an encyclopedia and will understand its purpose.

Time Required:

45 minutes

Provided Materials:

- "Kids Are Curious" (OER 1.3.1) PowerPoint
- "A Closer Look" (WS 1.3.1)—one per student
- "Encyclopedia 101" (OER 1.3.2) PowerPoint
- "Letters" (MN 1.3.1)—Cut out each section and place at tables prior to student arrival

Materials You Will Need to Obtain:

- A set of encyclopedias
- Projection device
- Pencils
- Laptop

Lesson Procedures:

Engagement:

1. Display the "Kids Are Curious" (OER 1.3.1) PowerPoint. The PowerPoint will automatically advance from slide to slide in the slideshow view. As students are viewing the slide show, explain that it is a natural curiosity to want to learn more about subjects and topics that interest us. Allow students time to view the slide show. Discuss with students how looking more closely at an image can provide more information. Ask students if the images prompted them to have questions about what they were viewing. Give students time to share some of their questions. Tell students that today they will be learning about a reference tool that will help answer some of the questions they have about the pictures they saw, or any question they may have about the world around them. Explain that students will be identifying a topic of interest and thinking about questions they may have about the topic.

Activity:

2. Place students into six groups and distribute copies of "A Closer Look" (WS 1.3.1). Ask students to draw a picture of anything they would like to learn more about that begins with one of the letters listed on their group "Letters" (MN 1.3.1) card. Students will use the lines below the magnifying glass on their worksheet to write questions they have about their topic.
3. Allow students time to complete "A Closer Look" (WS 1.3.1).
4. Create three columns on the board. Head the columns: person, place, thing.
5. Ask students to volunteer the topics they would like to learn more about from "A Closer Look" (WS 1.3.1). As each student gives their topic, write it on the board in the appropriate column. If any columns are left blank, ask students to provide an idea for that column.

6. Compliment the students on being curious about such a wide variety of topics.
7. Next, ask students to verbally share the questions they had for their topic.

Embedded AASL Skills Indicator: ___.___.___: _____

_____

8. Now that students have created a list of topics and several questions, ask students where they might go to locate information that will satisfy their curiosity by answering their question. Students may provide a variety of suggestions for where they can go for this type of information. Explain to students that today they will be using an encyclopedia to locate information about each of these topics. Tell students that encyclopedias contain information about famous people, places, things, and events.
9. Distribute the volumes of the selected encyclopedia chosen to use with the students making sure the volume letter correspond with the "Letters" (MN 1.3.1) that are on the table.
10. Display the "Encyclopedia 101" (OER 1.3.2) PowerPoint and tell students to use their encyclopedia to follow along and locate the various tools and text features discussed.
11. Follow the directions in the notes portion of the "Encyclopedia 101" (OER 1.3.2) PowerPoint.

Transition:

12. Instruct students to go back to their "A Closer Look" (WS 1.3.1) worksheet.

Activity:

Embedded AASL Skills Indicator: ___.___.___: _____

_____

Embedded AASL Dispositions in Action Indicator: ___.___.___: _____

_____

13. Allow students time to look up the topic they selected in the appropriate encyclopedia volume at their table.

Embedded AASL Responsibilities Indicator: ___.___.___: _____

_____

14. Give students time to explore their topic in the encyclopedia. If a student is unable to locate their topic, assist that student or explain why their topic might not be in the encyclopedia.

15. Discuss their findings as a class. Ask students to record the answers they found in question 1 of the self-assessment portion provided on their "A Closer Look" (WS 1.3.1) worksheet. If they were unable to locate their topic, ask for students to write a few sentences explaining why they think their topic could not be located.

CLASSROOM CONNECTIONS

Create a professional development brochure that explains how to navigate online encyclopedias to teachers. This way they will be more likely to use them in their classroom.

Closure:

Embedded AASL Self-Assessment Strategies: ___.___.___: _____

---

16. Ask for students to continue the completion of the self-assessment located on the back of their "A Closer Look" (WS 1.3.1) worksheet. Ask students to share their reflections with the class and discuss.
17. Show students where to find other encyclopedias that can be checked out from the media center. (Pull these books ahead of time so they are more readily accessible to students).

Evidence of Understanding:

Check that students are actively participating during the "Encyclopedia 101" (OER 1.3.2) PowerPoint. Assess students shared reflections for understanding.

Enrichment Using Technology:

Locate one or more online encyclopedia to use with students. Give students time to search and explore topics of interest. Options may include http://www.factmonster.com or an online subscription database purchased by the school system.

Extension:

1. Distribute copies of "My Entry" (EX 1.3.1) to students. Explain to students that an expert in the field of a particular topic writes each encyclopedia article. It takes many experts to create all of the entries that go into an encyclopedia. Ask students to think about a subject they are knowledgeable about and try creating their own encyclopedia entry complete with a picture, captions, and interesting factual information.

Suggested Modifications:

For the "A Closer Look" (WS 1.3.1) worksheet, have students in need of modifications write just one question to go along with their picture instead of several questions. Be sure and pair students with reading difficulties with stronger readers when sharing the "Encyclopedia 101" (OER 1.3.2) PowerPoint.

A CLOSER LOOK

Name: _____

Directions: Inside the magnifying glass, draw a picture of a topic you'd like to learn more about. In the spaces below, write down some questions you would like answered about that specific topic.

Questions I have about my topic:

_____

_____

_____

_____

_____

SELF-ASSESSMENT

1. When you looked in the encyclopedia, did it provide you with an answer to the question(s) you had? If it did, provide the answer. If it did not provide you with an answer, explain why you think your topic is not in the encyclopedia.

_____

_____

_____

_____

2. What are some other questions you have about the topic you selected?

_____

_____

_____

_____

3. Is there another topic you would like to use the encyclopedia to learn more about?

_____

_____

_____

_____

4. What are some other places you can look to find accurate and reliable information about your topic?

_____

_____

_____

_____

5. Would you use an encyclopedia again in the future? Why or why not?

_____

_____

_____

_____

LETTERS

```
┌─────────────────────────┐
│ Table 1                 │
│                         │
│ A                       │
│                         │
│ B                       │
│                         │
│ C                       │
└─────────────────────────┘
```

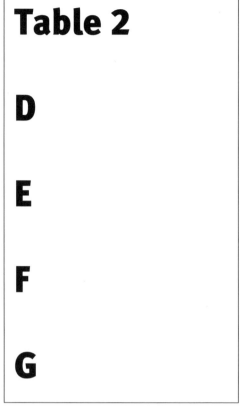

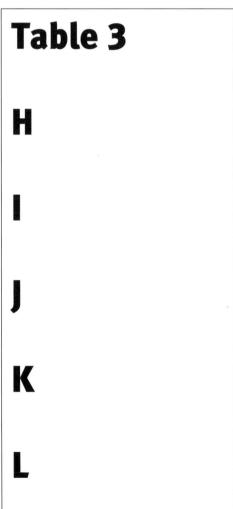

Table 4
M
N
O
P
Q
R

Table 6
U
V
W
X
Y
Z

MY ENTRY

Name: _____

Entry Name: _____   _____

_____   _____

_____   _____

_____   _____

_____   _____

_____   _____

_____

_____   ┌─────────────────────────┐
_____   │   │
_____   │   │
_____   │   │
_____   │   │
_____   │   │
_____   └─────────────────────────┘

Caption: _____

_____

Works Cited

_____

_____

_____

3RD-GRADE LESSONS

LESSON 2: ENCYCLOPEDIA TRIVIA

Coordinate! Students review text feature skills as well as how to access information in an encyclopedia. *Coordinate* with the classroom teacher by offering to share the "Encyclopedia Trivia" (OER 1.3.3) PowerPoint. The teacher could use the PowerPoint as a template to make their own trivia-style games for the classroom or the teacher can play the game to reinforce encyclopedia skills.

Cooperate! After the completion of this lesson, students should be comfortable with using encyclopedias to locate information for academic pursuits, and they should have an understanding of how they can use encyclopedias to satisfy a need or curiosity for more information. *Cooperate* with the classroom teacher by offering to share the completed "Student Trivia" (WS 1.3.2) worksheets. The teacher can use these student-generated questions as a class warm-up for practice using encyclopedias and accessing information.

Lesson Plan

Integrated Goals:

Language Arts

Standard 8. Students use a variety of technological and information resources (e.g., libraries, databases, computer networks, video) to gather and synthesize information and to create and communicate knowledge.

Library Media

AASL 21st Century Standards

Standard 1: Inquire, think critically, and gain knowledge.

Essential Questions:

How can encyclopedias help you answer basic information questions?
How can text features help you find information in an encyclopedia?

Desired Understandings:

Students will understand:

How to locate information in an encyclopedia to answer general information questions.
How to use text features when searching for information in an encyclopedia.

Integrated Objectives:

- Students will learn how to use an encyclopedia and will understand its purpose.

Time Required:

45 minutes

Provided Materials:

- "Encyclopedia Trivia" (OER 1.3.3) PowerPoint—add in your own name as the host

  *Note—If you choose to use the applause button, you will need to download the applause sound effect listed in the resources section of the PowerPoint, or locate and add your own applause.

- "Student Trivia" (WS 1.3.2)—one per student—Save these completed trivia cards for further encyclopedia practice in future classes.

Materials You Will Need to Obtain:

- Computer
- Projection device
- Paper and pencils for each team
- Set of encyclopedias

Optional Materials:

- Bookmarks, stickers, or small prizes for the winning team if you wish to distribute prizes

Lesson Procedures:

Engagement:

1. Display the first slide of the "Encyclopedia Trivia" (OER 1.3.3) PowerPoint. Tell students that today they will participate in a Jeopardy-style game. They will use the information they learned in the last class to answer questions about encyclopedias, and then they will create their own trivia questions and answers for students to use in a trivia game for future encyclopedia use practice.

Activity:

2. Divide the class into 4–6 teams.
3. Display slide 3 of the "Encyclopedia Trivia" (OER 1.3.3) PowerPoint.
4. Point out and read each of the trivia categories. Tell students that each question has to do with encyclopedias in some way, and students should work with their teammates to identify the correct answer.

Embedded AASL Skills Indicator: ___.___.___: _____

_____

5. Once students have discussed their answer with their teammates, one person from the team should raise their hand to answer. If the answer is correct, the team will earn the number of points listed on the question. If you chose to activate the "Applause" feature, the "Applause" button at the top of the home page of the trivia game will give teams a round of applause for giving the correct answer.

6. As you go through the game and students answer each question, elaborate on why answers are correct or incorrect. You may also want to make it a requirement that students must give their answers in the form of a question.
7. If a team is incorrect in their answer, points will not be taken away, and another team will have an opportunity to answer. Play continues until a team has guessed the correct answer, or until the library media specialist decides it is time to give the correct answer. Keep track of the points for each team in a prominent area of the room. The team who answers correctly can choose the next category.
8. Once all of the questions have been answered, students should determine how many of their points they are willing to risk for the final trivia question. Once each team has decided on a point value to risk, write down this amount on a piece of paper so that other teams in the class cannot see what each team risked.
9. Give the teams two minutes to think about the final trivia question, and then have the teams record their answers to the final question. When the two minutes are up, ask each team to share their answers and then share the point value each team risked. Tally up the scores. The team with the highest amount of points is declared the winner.

Transition:

10. Congratulate all of the teams on a job well done.
11. Remind students that encyclopedias are often used to find quick answers to questions, to begin research, and to learn more about a general topic.
12. Tell students that they will be using the encyclopedia to locate information on a topic that interests them in order to create a trivia question and answer. The completed trivia cards will be used during library media classes to practice using the encyclopedias to locate information.
13. Distribute the "Student Trivia" (WS 1.3.2) worksheets to each student.

Activity:

14. Read aloud the directions on the "Student Trivia" (WS 1.3.2) worksheet and clarify any questions students may have regarding the activity.

Embedded AASL Skills Indicator: ___.___.___: _____

_____

Embedded AASL Dispositions in Action Indicator: ___.___.___: _____

_____

Embedded AASL Responsibilities Indicator: ___.___.___: _____

_____

15. Allow students time to complete the activity.

16. Once students have completed the question portion of their "Student Trivia" (WS 1.3.2) worksheet, ask students to answer the two self-assessment questions at the bottom of the page.

Closure:

17. Ask for a few students in the class to share what they recorded in their self-assessment.
18. Collect the "Student Trivia" (WS 1.3.2) worksheets from the students. If time permits, ask students a question taken from one of the completed "Student Trivia" (WS 1.3.2) cards and see if the class can locate the answer in the encyclopedia.

Evidence of Understanding:

Observe students' ability to answer each question to determine whether they understand how to use an encyclopedia. Review as needed. Grade the "Student Trivia" (WS 1.3.2) worksheets for completion and understanding.

Technology Integration:

Technology

NETS-S

3. Research and Information Fluency

Students apply digital tools to gather, evaluate, and use information. Students:

  b. locate, organize, analyze, evaluate, synthesize, and ethically use information from a variety of sources and media.

  Instead of or in addition to using print encyclopedias for students to complete the "Student Trivia" (WS 1.3.2) worksheets, give students an opportunity to use online encyclopedias to complete this information. Options could include http://www.factmonster.com or an online subscription database purchased by the school system.

Extension:

1. Distribute copies of "Try Your Own Trivia" (EX 1.3.2). Give students an opportunity to come up with their own encyclopedia trivia questions. You may choose to add or update these questions into the "Encyclopedia Trivia" (OER 1.3.3) Power-Point.

Suggested Modifications:

When dividing your class into teams, keep in mind the various reading levels of your students and be sure to place stronger readers into groups with struggling readers.

STUDENT TRIVIA

Name: _____

Directions: Think of a topic that interests you and look it up in the encyclopedia. After reading about your topic, create a trivia question that you could ask your classmate.

For example: If I looked up dinosaurs, I could ask a question such as, "Tyrannosaurus Rex lived how many million years ago?" Be sure and include your answer as well as the encyclopedia volume and article you used to find your information. Once the whole class has completed their own question, there will be plenty of trivia cards for students to use to practice using encyclopedias.

Trivia question: _____

_____

_____

Trivia answer: _____

_____

This information was found . . .

_____

_____

_____

SELF-ASSESSMENT

1. Do you think your trivia question would be difficult for others to answer of they did not have an encyclopedia to use? Explain.

_____

_____

_____

2. What have you contributed to help others learn more?

_____

_____

_____

TRY YOUR OWN TRIVIA

Name: _____

Directions: Create your own trivia questions and answers for an encyclopedia trivia game!

Q.

Q.

A.

A.

Working in Collaboration

Collaborate! True collaboration requires both the library media specialist and the classroom teacher to share in the design of integrated instruction. Collaboration provides you with an excellent opportunity to design inquiry-based learning activities. Here are some ideas for collaborating with the classroom teachers.

3rd Grade: Language Arts

Essential Question: How can encyclopedias enhance my experience with literature?

- Have students read a literary text of historical fiction, realistic fiction, or another genre with events or subject matter that could be explored in an encyclopedia. Give students an opportunity to explore both the creative and nonfiction side of literature.
- Challenge students to learn about a subject of interest to them in the encyclopedia. Using the information they found as background knowledge, students could write their own realistic fiction or historical fiction story.

For further information, please visit
www.destinationcollaboration.com

4TH-GRADE LESSONS

LESSON 1: INFORMATION STATION

Coordinate! Playing games with students, such as the one in this lesson with the "Information Station Game" (OER 1.4.2) PowerPoint, is a great way to engage and motivate students to learn new skills and concepts. *Coordinate* with the classroom teacher by sharing the template for this board-style game to be used in the classroom for a variety of other desired learning goals.

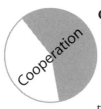

Cooperate! After students complete this lesson, *cooperate* with the classroom teacher by offering to extend this learning experience. Offer to assist the classroom teacher by helping students locate information for an upcoming class project using print and online encyclopedias as a starting point for their research. Consider allowing students extra time in the media center to locate encyclopedia entries based upon their assigned subject.

Lesson Plan

Integrated Goals:

Language Arts

Standard 8. Students use a variety of technological and information resources (e.g., libraries, databases, computer networks, video) to gather and synthesize information and to create and communicate knowledge.

Technology

NETS-S

3. Research and Information Fluency

Students apply digital tools to gather, evaluate, and use information. Students:

b. locate, organize, analyze, evaluate, synthesize, and ethically use information from a variety of sources and media.

Library Media

AASL 21st Century Standards

  Standard 1: Inquire, think critically, and gain knowledge.

Essential Questions:

  How can online and print encyclopedias help to satisfy an information need?

Desired Understandings:

Students will understand:

How to navigate print and online encyclopedias.

Similarities and differences between online and print encyclopedias.

CLASSROOM CONNECTIONS

Gather information about what students are learning in their classrooms as you prepare to teach this lesson. Feel free to substitute the trivia questions in the game with questions that students may need to know for an upcoming test or project.

Integrated Objectives:

- Students will determine the similarities and differences between print and online encyclopedias.
- Students will use encyclopedias in multiple formats to locate information.

Time Required:

45 minutes

Provided Materials:

- "Colorful Facts" (WS 1.4.1)—one per student
- "Information Station Game" (OER 1.4.2) PowerPoint
- "Game Directions" (TRS 1.4.1)
- "Team Stars" (OMN 1.4.2)—one star per student
- "Information Station Trivia Questions" (ORS 1.4.1) PowerPoint—Print four copies of the questions by selecting the "print handouts 4 slides per page" option, cut out each slide, and laminate if possible. Place the slides in order, and hole punch them in the upper left-hand corner so that they can slide over a "book ring" for use during the game.
- "Information Station Trivia Answers" (OTRS 1.4.2) PowerPoint—Print one copy for teacher use. You may also wish to print these by selecting the "print handouts 4 slides per page" option, and then cut out each slide and place them in a container so that you can select the questions at random.
- "Information Answer Sheet" (RS 1.4.1)—one per team
- OPTIONAL—"Fact Finder" (OER 1.4.1) PowerPoint—Print out the "notes" view for directions on how to instruct students throughout the PowerPoint.
- OPTIONAL—"Magic Fact Finder" (MN 1.4.1)—Print onto cardstock and affix to a ruler or just substitute a wand or pointer if available.
- "Colorful Facts" (OEWS 1.4.1) *online material

Materials You Will Need to Obtain:

- Computer
- Projection device
- Computer access for the entire class
- Access to an online encyclopedia
- Ruler
- Colored pencils and/or crayons for student use
- A set of encyclopedias
- At least five book rings to keep the trivia questions together

Optional Materials:

- Computer remote to use with the optional "Fact Finder" (OER 1.4.1) PowerPoint

Lesson Procedures:

Engagement:

1. Ask students to recall the tool they should use when locating general information about a topic (encyclopedias).

2. Distribute copies of "Colorful Facts" (WS 1.4.1) to each student. Explain to students that the worksheet will assess their ability to use text features, a necessary basic skill when using encyclopedias. Give students time to complete the worksheet.

3. Review the answers with students and determine whether students are ready to move forward, or if they need additional practice using the encyclopedias. If a review is necessary, use the *optional* activity included below. If not, proceed to the activity.

- *Optional*—If students need additional reinforcement regarding encyclopedias, share the optional "Fact Finder" (OER 1.4.1) PowerPoint and use the "Magic Fact Finder" (MN 1.4.1) to go along with it. Please note—if this option is used, the unit may need to be extended.

Activity:

4. Tell students that encyclopedias are a good place to look for basic facts about a wide variety of topics.

5. Display the home search page of the online encyclopedia selected for use with this lesson.

6. Demonstrate how to navigate through the site by using keywords to search for various subjects and topics.

Embedded AASL Skills Indicator: ___.___.___: _____

_____

7. Explain to students that they will be working in groups using both print and online encyclopedias to play a scavenger hunt trivia game.

Transition:

8. Use the "Team Stars" (OMN 1.4.2) to divide students into four teams.

9. Give each team access to some volumes from a set of encyclopedias (split it up so that each team has an equal number of volumes) as well as access to online encyclopedias.

Activity:

10. Display the "Information Station Game" (OER 1.4.2) and explain how to play the game by using the "Game Directions" (TRS 1.4.1).

11. Distribute a copy of the "Information Station Trivia Questions" (ORS 1.4.1) to each group to use as a reference.

12. Distribute the "Information Answer Sheet" (RS 1.4.1) to each team for recording their answers.

Embedded AASL Responsibilities Indicator: ___.___.___: _____

_____

Embedded AASL Dispositions in Action Indicator: ___.___.___: _____

_____

13. Play the "Information Station Game" (OER 1.4.2) with students. Review the answers and how they were found as game play continues.

Closure:

Embedded AASL Self-Assessment Strategies: ___.___.___: _____

_____

14. On the last page of the "Information Answer Sheet" (RS 1.4.1), students are asked to share the similarities and differences between online and print encyclopedias, and which they liked using more and why. Ask students to discuss the questions with the other members of their team, and to write one comprehensive group answer.
15. Ask for teams to share their self-assessments with the class.

Evidence of Understanding:

Collect and check "Colorful Facts" (WS 1.4.1) for student understanding. Collect the "Information Answer Sheet" (RS 1.4.1) and check that all teams were successful in their searches for information.

Technology Integration:

Technology

NETS-S

6. Technology Operations and Concepts

Students demonstrate a sound understanding of technology concepts, systems, and operations. Students:

a. understand and use technology systems.
1. Use the electronic version of "Colorful Facts" (OEWS 1.4.1) for your activity instead of the paper, pencil, and crayon version. In order to use this option, students will need access to the electronic worksheet on a computer. In this version, students will "drag" the colored circles and rectangles over the appropriate parts of the entry.

Extension:

1. Challenge students to write original trivia questions from the encyclopedia that can be saved and used with another class.

Suggested Modifications:

Print copies of the modified "Information Station Trivia" (OMOD 1.4.1) for students who might need extra help in selecting the important keywords to look up in the encyclopedia. You may also wish to pair these students with stronger readers or computer users in the class.

COLORFUL FACTS

Name: _____

Directions: Read the encyclopedia entry below. Then follow the directions at the bottom of the page.

Robots

Robots are machines that can do many different tasks automatically. The word "robot" is Czech for drudgery. Robots are excellent to use for completing various tasks that may be too dangerous or difficult for humans to do. Robots are also now being used for jobs that are very basic and easy to do for humans.

Jobs for robots

- Assembling electronics
- Welding
- Wrapping ice cream bars
- Drilling
- Making plastic containers

Humans desire robots for certain jobs because robots follow directions very well. Robots perform their job because someone *programmed* them to do so. Robots are given a set of instructions, which are stored in a computer, or control center for the robot. The robot then follows that set of instructions to complete the job.

Many times, robots in movies are made to look human like. In reality, most robots are made to stay in just one place and have a special arm that is used to pick up and move objects. A few robots can "see" with built-in television cameras and have special touch sensors. These types of robots have been used to explore areas that have been off limits to humans , such as the planet Mars and parts of the ocean that are too deep for human travel.

Mobile robot

Take a look at rhe Tech Museum of Innovation for more information.

http:// www.thetech.org/exhibits/online/robotics/universal/index.html

1. Underline the URL in red.
2. Circle the italicized word in blue.
3. Draw a yellow arrow pointing to the bulleted list.
4. Place a purple star next to the bolded word.
5. Draw a black box around the entry.
6. Place a green X next to the caption.
7. Draw a brown triangle to the right of the picture.

Sources

Kazerounian, Kazem. "Robots." World Book Online. World Book Online Reference Center. 2008. Web. 25 May 2008.
<http://www.worldbookonline.com/>.
Winkvist, S. LIDAR equipped mobile robot. Photograph. 3 Mar. 2008 Web. 28 Dec. 2008.
<http://commons.wikimedia.org/wiki/File:LIDAR_equipped_mobile_robot.jpg>.

GAME DIRECTIONS

1. Divide the class into four teams.

2. Assign each team one of the colored stars from "Team Stars" (OMN 1.4.2) (green, red, blue, or yellow). You can print and make copies of the stars ahead of time and have students choose a star from a jar in order to place them in their groups randomly.

3. Once the encyclopedias and computers have been distributed (you may wish to do this at the beginning of the class in order to save time), display the "Information Station Game" (OER 1.4.2) for all students to see. You will want to put this on "slide view," not "slide show." Students see a larger picture with the slide view, and you can still manipulate the pieces on the board. If you set the PowerPoint to "slide show," you will not be able to click on and move the pieces on the board. On your tool bar at the top of the page, you can select "View" and then "Slide" to get to the "slide view."

4. Tell students that in order to win the game, they must use both online and print encyclopedias to answer trivia questions. *NOTE* Trivia questions will need to be printed ahead of time from the "Information Station Trivia Questions" (ORS 1.4.2) PowerPoint. For each trivia question they answer correctly, they will advance a space on the board. The first team to reach the finish line first wins.

5. Explain that you will select a trivia question and read it aloud to the class. Trivia questions will also be given to the students ahead of time in a flip book format. Students should flip to the trivia question you select to begin looking up the answer to the question.

6. Allow students time to locate the answer. Once students locate the correct answer, they must write down the correct answer on their "Information Answer Sheet" (RS 1.4.2), and have a student from the team raise their hand. The team to locate the correct answer first gets to either move forward two spaces *or* move forward one space and send an opponent back one space. After a team has located the correct answer, give an additional three minutes for the other teams to locate the answer as well. If the other teams can locate and write down the correct answer within the three minutes, they may move forward one space on the board. If not, they stay where they are on the board. Be sure and tell students that they *must not* move ahead to other questions until you have selected the next question.

Moving pieces on the board is simple, just click, drag, and drop the appropriate colored star into the appropriate space on the board. Play continues until the class ends or until a team reaches the finish.

INFORMATION ANSWER SHEET

Team color: _____

Student names:

_____

_____

Question # _____

Answer

_____

_____

Question # _____

Answer

_____

_____

Question # _____

Answer

_____

_____

Question # _____

Answer

_____

_____

Question # _____

Answer

_____

_____

Question # _____

Answer

_____

_____

Question # _____

Answer
_____

_____

Question # _____

Answer
_____

_____

Question # _____

Answer
_____

_____

Question # _____

Answer
_____

_____

Question # _____

Answer
_____

_____

Question # _____

Answer
_____

_____

Question # _____

Answer
_____

_____

Question # _____

Answer

_____

_____

Question # _____

Answer

_____

_____

Question # _____

Answer

_____

_____

Question # _____

Answer

_____

_____

Question # _____

Answer

_____

_____

Question # _____

Answer

_____

_____

Question # _____

Answer

_____

_____

TEAM ASSESSMENT

What were some similarities between print and online encyclopedias?

_____

_____

_____

_____

_____

_____

_____

What were some differences between print and online encyclopedias?

_____

_____

_____

_____

_____

_____

_____

Which did you prefer to use? Why?

_____

_____

_____

_____

_____

_____

_____

MAGIC FACT FINDER

Fact Finder

Point this star at the answer you select,
magic will happen if your answer is correct!

4TH-GRADE LESSONS

LESSON 2: ENCYCLOPEDIA RETAIL

Coordinate! Students will enjoy creating something that is of interest to them in this lesson. Consider *coordinating* with the classroom teacher to use this lesson involving interactive online animals as an opportunity to discuss online safety with students and parents. Also consider teaching this lesson when students are learning about animal habitats or biomes of the world.

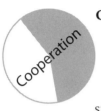

Cooperate! Share this lesson with the classroom teacher prior to beginning the lesson with students. The classroom teacher may have an upcoming assignment for students involving animal habitats or endangered species that could be used as the basis for this lesson. *Cooperate* with the classroom teacher to create a more appropriate list of animals that complements what students are learning about in the classroom.

Lesson Plan

Integrated Goals:

Language Arts

Standard 8. Students use a variety of technological and information resources (e.g., libraries, databases, computer networks, video) to gather and synthesize information and to create and communicate knowledge.

Standard 12. Students use spoken, written, and visual language to accomplish their own purposes (e.g., for learning, enjoyment, persuasion, and the exchange of information).

Technology

NETS-S

3. Research and Information Fluency

Students apply digital tools to gather, evaluate, and use information. Students:

b. locate, organize, analyze, evaluate, synthesize, and ethically use information from a variety of sources and media.

Library Media

AASL 21st Century Standards

Standard 1: Inquire, think critically, and gain knowledge.

Essential Questions:

How can online and print encyclopedias help to satisfy an information need?

Desired Understandings:

Students will understand:

How to navigate print and online encyclopedias.

How to interpret information from print and online encyclopedias to complete a project.

Integrated Objectives:

- Students will use encyclopedias in multiple formats to locate information.
- Students will use animal facts to design and create a package for a "digi-animal."

Time Required:

45 minutes

Provided Materials:

- "Animal List" (RS 1.4.2)
- "Digi-Animal Fact Sheet" (WS 1.4.3)—one per student
- "Digi-Animal Package Template" (WS 1.4.2)—one per student—copy this worksheet onto 11x16 paper and increase the size by 150% to allow adequate space for students to record and illustrate their ideas.
- "Digi-Animal Rubric" (RS 1.4.3)—one per student
- "Package Planning" (OER 1.4.3) PowerPoint

Materials You Will Need to Obtain:

- Computer
- Projection device
- A set of encyclopedias
- Computers for student use with access to http://www.factmonster.com or an online subscription database purchased by the school system
- Art supplies such as crayons, markers, colored pencils, and scissors

Lesson Procedures:

Engagement:

1. Display a Web site for a virtual pet such as Webkinz, http://www.webkinz.com.
2. Ask students to raise their hands if they have ever played with a virtual pet before and share how it works with the class (e.g., caring for it, playing with it, grooming it, feeding it, etc.).
3. Tell students that they will be designing a package for a pet that could be placed online. Explain that similar to Webkinz, students will need to advertise their pet by creating a package. The class will vote on which animal they think will be most likely to be adopted based on the package design and information advertising the pet.

Activity:

4. Tell students that their job will be to use both print and online encyclopedias to select an entry about an animal of their choosing, and then they will create

> **DISCUSSION OPPORTUNITY**
>
> Use this lesson as an opportunity to discuss online safety with students. Because digital and online games are becoming more and more popular with students, students need a constant reminder of appropriate and safe online behavior.

a product package to advertise their new online interactive digital animal. The package should not only give basic facts about the animal and its habitat but it should also include directions on how to care for the animal and tips for keeping the online pet healthy and happy.

5. Display the "Animal List" (RS 1.4.2) and ask that students select an animal from the list that they would like to know more about.
6. Display the "Digi-Animal Fact Sheet" (WS 1.4.3) and demonstrate to students how to use both the print and online encyclopedia to record notes onto the sheet.
7. Distribute copies of the "Digi-Animal Fact Sheet" (WS 1.4.3) to each student.

Embedded AASL Skills Indicator: ___.___.___: _____

_____

Embedded AASL Responsibilities Indicator: ___.___.___: _____

_____

8. Remind students that in the previous lesson, they discussed the differences between an online encyclopedia and a print encyclopedia. Have students recall which type of encyclopedia they preferred to use, and have them share why.
9. Give students access to both print and online encyclopedias and allow students time to look up their animal and read about it from the encyclopedia source they identified as being the best for them to use.
10. Give students time to complete the "Digi-Animal Fact Sheet" (WS 1.4.3) for the animal they have chosen to research.

Embedded AASL Skills Indicator: ___.___.___: _____

_____

Transition:

11. Explain to students that many toys played with by boys and girls are based on something real. The students will use the facts they learn to create a believable virtual toy that children would want to play with and learn more about.

Activity:

12. Distribute the "Digi-Animal Rubric" (RS 1.4.3) and go over the requirements of the assignment. Students can use this rubric to assist them as they complete their project.
13. Distribute the "Digi-Animal Package Template" (WS 1.4.2).
14. Read the directions and explain to students how to complete the assignment.
15. In addition to verbally explaining the directions, use the "Package Planning" (OER 1.4.3) PowerPoint to illustrate and demonstrate how to properly complete the "Digi-Animal Package Template" (WS 1.4.2).

16. Give students time to complete the written portion of the assignment and then distribute art supplies for students to decorate and assemble their product box.
17. Give students time to complete their projects.

Closure:

Embedded AASL Self-Assessment Strategies: ___.___.___: _____

18. Ask students to compare their completed project with the "Digi-Animal Rubric" (RS 1.4.3) and complete the questions on the back to record how they think they did on the project.
19. Ask students to share their complete digi-animal package with the class and explain their project.

Evidence of Understanding:

Assist students throughout their completion of the project to ensure they understand the assignment. Collect and grade the "Digi-Animal Package Template" (WS 1.4.2) using the "Digi-Animal Rubric" (RS 1.4.3).

Enrichment Using Technology:

1. Take pictures of the student projects and post them to a blog site. Students can use the blog site to comment and provide feedback to one another's work.

Extension:

1. Students will find that the encyclopedia articles only give a general overview of the animal they researched. Ask students to record some questions they still have about the animal they researched. Then provide students with access to other books, articles, and Web sites about animals so they can learn more about the animal they researched.

Suggested Modifications:

Depending on the ability level of the students, modify this activity by placing students into groups of two or three to conduct research together and creatively complete the project.

21ST CENTURY SKILL

Once you have completed the unit, consider having students create an infomercial to advertise their digi-animal. Videotape the infomercials and share on the school televised morning announcements (if available) or the school Web site. This activity will give students an opportunity to collaborate, communicate, and create a media product to share with a larger community of learners—all 21st-century learning skills.

ANIMAL LIST

antelope	ibis	quail
ape	iguana	quetzal
bear	jackal	raccoon
beaver	jack rabbit	reindeer
camel	katydid	sheep
clam	killdeer	spider
dingo	ladybug	takin
dog	lobster	turtle
elephant	mouse	uakari
ermine	muskrat	vampire bat
fox	narwhal	viper
frog	nuthatch	walrus
giraffe	octopus	whale
goat	otter	yak
hermit crab	paca	yellow jacket
horse	polar bear	zebra

DIGI-ANIMAL FACT SHEET

Created by: _____

Animal description

- (Size) _____

_____

- (Color) _____

_____

- (Weight) _____

_____

- (Other) _____

_____

Animal picture

- (Name of Digi-Animal)

_____

Animal needs

- (Diet)_____

_____

- (Habitat)_____

_____

- (Exercise)_____

_____

- (Important facts for the care of this

pet)_____

_____

Accessory ideas

Record ideas of items that could be included

with your Digi-Animal that would help

someone better understand the type of care

this animal needs._____

_____

_____

_____

_____

_____

Source citation (where did you find your information?):_____

_____

_____

_____

_____

DIGI-ANIMAL PACKAGE TEMPLATE

Project directions: Complete the product package below to demonstrate what you learned from your encyclopedia research. Complete each of the numbered sections, creatively displaying the following information.

Section 1: The top of your box should include the name of your product.
Section 2: This bottom portion of the box is for you to write your name.
Section 3: This portion of the box should include facts about your animal, such as where this animal lives, what it looks like, what it eats, and so forth.
Section 4: This is the front of your box and should include the name and picture of your animal.
Sections 5 & 6: These side areas of your box should explain what you have learned about your animal. These understandings can be demonstrated by including accessories with your Digi-Animal that relate to what it will need to be taken well care of. However the reason why these accessories were chosen must be clearly explained and also why they are important.

Assembly Directions:
1. Cut out the perimeter of the box on the solid black lines.
2. Cut any remaining black lines on the box flaps.
3. Neatly fold each of the dotted lines on the box.
4. Assemble the box.
5. Place glue on the two parts of the box with the words GLUE written on it.
6. Press gently, and hold the bottom and side of the box together and let the glue set.

GLUE

GLUE

4

6

1

3

2

5

DIGI-ANIMAL RUBRIC

Expectations	Not met (1)	Almost there (2)	Great job! (3)
The toy package should include facts from research, which describe the animal's habitat, what the animal looks like, the diet and size of the animal.	The student did not include facts related to the animal they researched.	The student included a few facts, but did not completely satisfy the expectations.	The student provided enough facts for readers to develop new understanding from the student's project.
Students should include their own ideas into the toy package to show they have made connections to what they learned. These ideas can be in the form of the toy "accessories" that would assist with pet care.	The student was limited in the ideas they included. The connections made by the student were unclear.	The student made an attempt to create connections from the encyclopedia article to their package.	The students successfully demonstrated what they learned by including several accessory suggestions with their package, and they supported each suggestion with evidence to show why the accessory was important.
Students should show evidence of creativity through their package design and descriptions.	The student completed the assignment, but no creativity was evident.	The student made an attempt to decorate their package and include interesting descriptions of the product for the reader.	The students package demonstrated creativity through its attractive decoration and design and interesting descriptions and slogans.
Students should include a picture that relates to the animal they researched.	The students did not include a picture.	The students included a picture, but it is not apparent how this picture relates to the animal they researched.	Students created a picture that can easily be associated with the animal researched.
The work is neat, complete, and demonstrates proper spelling, punctuation, and grammar usage.	Because of the students' punctuation, spelling, and grammar mistakes, the project was difficult to interpret.	The students made an effort to include proper spelling, punctuation, and grammar. There were only a few mistakes.	The students used proper punctuation, spelling, and grammar throughout the project.
The encyclopedia article used to gather information for this project should be cited on the toy package.	The student made no attempt to create a citation.	The student cited their source, but the citation was incomplete.	The student successfully cited the encyclopedia used for the project and included all necessary information.
Total points			

SELF-ASSESSMENT QUESTIONS

1. Were there any questions you had about your animal that the encyclopedia didn't answer?

_____

_____

_____

_____

2. What other questions do you have?

_____

_____

_____

_____

3. How would you use encyclopedias again in the future?

_____

_____

_____

_____

4. Would you be more likely to use print or online encyclopedias? Why?

_____

_____

_____

_____

5. How did the rubric assist you in the completion of your project?

_____

_____

_____

_____

Working in Collaboration

Collaborate! True collaboration requires both the library media specialist and the classroom teacher to share in the design of integrated instruction. Collaboration provides you with an excellent opportunity to design inquiry-based learning activities. Here are some ideas for collaborating with the classroom teachers.

4th Grade: Science

Essential Question: How do plants and animals help each other in Earth's many biomes?

- Create an interactive biome using Google Sites. Using encyclopedias, students can work in small groups to research an animal or plant from a selected biome. Students can post what they learned and share links to more information on the site. Place a twist on the activity by having students write a blog entry from the point of view of a particular animal. The entries could be organized by biome. Students may even see some interesting food cycle patterns from this activity.

For further information, please visit
www.destinationcollaboration.com

5TH-GRADE LESSONS

LESSON 1: ENCYCLOPEDIA DISASTER

Coordinate! Parents may be unaware that elementary school students are responsible for knowing about source reliability. Use this lesson as an opportunity to *coordinate* with the classroom teacher and discuss possible ways in which parents can be made more aware of the importance of using reliable resources with students. If the school or district subscribes to databases, this would be a perfect opportunity to demonstrate to parents how to access and use these tools. Offer to give the classroom teacher information about how to access reliable databases subscribed to by the school system for the classroom or grade-level newsletter.

Cooperate! Check with the classroom teacher to see when teaching about natural disasters occurs in their curriculum. *Cooperate* by offering to assist the class in designing an appropriate research question based on what the students want to know about natural disasters. Teach the lessons to coincide with when students are studying natural disasters or a similar topic in their classroom.

Lesson Plan

Integrated Goals:

Language Arts

Standard 12. Students use spoken, written, and visual language to accomplish their own purposes (e.g., for learning, enjoyment, persuasion, and the exchange of information)

Science in Personal and Social Perspectives

Content Standard F: Grades 5–8

As a result of activities in grades 5–8, all students should develop understanding of

- Natural hazards

Library Media

AASL 21st Century Standards

Standard 1: Inquire, think critically, and gain knowledge.
Standard 2: Draw conclusions, make informed decisions, apply knowledge to new situations, and create new knowledge.

Essential Questions:

How does the use of multiple resources assist in completing more thorough research?
When is it appropriate to use Wikipedia?

Desired Understandings:

Students will understand:

Why it is important to cross-check more than one resource when conducting research.
The differences between traditional encyclopedias and Wikipedia.
How to tell when a source is "reliable."

Integrated Objectives:

- Students will use online encyclopedias, Wikipedia, and books to research natural disasters and a natural disaster in history.
- Students will determine the reliability of free resources such as Wikipedia.

Time Required:

45 minutes

Provided Materials:

- "Disaster Topic List" (MN 1.5.1)—make three copies, cut out each disaster, and place in a container for students to select
- "Disaster Notes" (WS 1.5.1)—one per group

Materials You Will Need to Obtain:

- Computer
- Projection device
- Pencils
- Computers for student use with access to World Book Online or another reliable online encyclopedia, and Wikipedia
- Access to articles about natural disasters
- Books about natural disasters
- A video clip about a natural disaster

Lesson Procedures:

Engagement:

1. Show students a video clip about a natural disaster. This clip can be taken from a DVD you already have in your collection, one of the natural disaster videos found on the National Geographic Web site (http://video.nationalgeographic.com/video/) or the subscription database Discovery Streaming (http://streaming.discoveryeducation.com/).

Activity:

2. After showing students the natural disaster video clip, explain that they will be creating their own news story about a natural disaster that occurred in history.
3. Remind students that an encyclopedia is a great place to go as a first stop for completing research on any general topic.
4. Explain to students they will work in groups of three to locate facts about their natural disaster.
5. Have students randomly select a natural disaster from the container. The container holds choices from the "Disaster Topic List" (MN 1.5.1), which were previously copied and cut apart. This will determine group assignments. Ask that students find and sit with other members of their group.

Transition:

6. Distribute the "Disaster Notes" (WS 1.5.1) to each group of students.

Activity:

7. Display the search page for the online encyclopedia you have chosen to use with your students, and select a disaster topic from the "Disaster Topic List" (MN 1.5.1) to search.

8. Using the chosen sample topic, demonstrate ways that the online encyclopedia can be searched and properly used. Explain to students that articles in a reputable encyclopedia are researched by experts in that field of study and are confirmed with other sources before being published.

Embedded AASL Skills Indicator: ___.___.___: _____

_____

Embedded AASL Skills Indicator: ___.___.___: _____

_____

Embedded AASL Dispositions in Action Indicator: ___.___.___: _____

_____

Embedded AASL Responsibilities Indicator: ___.___.___: _____

_____

9. Next display the Wikipedia search page (http://www.wikipedia.org/) and search the same topic again. Explain to students that while Wikipedia is a form of an online encyclopedia, the content can be changed and edited virtually by anyone in the world. Even though users are supposed to include supporting documentation regarding the information they post to Wikipedia, it is always important to cross-check several resources prior to using information found on Wikipedia for a project. Explain that this is also true of print resources, including print encyclopedias, due to rapidly changing information. Show the books available on natural disasters that you have set-aside prior to the start of the class. Students will also be expected to confirm their research with information from the books.

10. Explain that students will have access to the online encyclopedia as well as the Wikipedia site and that they should use both in order to complete their "Disaster Notes" (WS 1.5.1).

11. Show students that on the "Disaster Notes" (WS 1.5.1) worksheet, there is a space to record information from the online encyclopedia as well as Wikipedia.

Embedded AASL Dispositions in Action Indicator: ___.___.___: _____

---

12. Students should take turns in both the research and recording of information.
13. Provide each group with access to an online encyclopedia and Wikipedia, as well as book resources to cross-check information about their natural disaster.

Embedded AASL Skills Indicator: ___.___.___: _____

---

14. Allow students time to locate and record the information onto their "Disaster Notes" (WS 1.5.1).

Closure:

Embedded AASL Self-Assessment Strategies: ___.___.___: _____

---

15. Ask students to discuss the last two questions of the "Disaster Notes" (WS 1.5.1) with the other members of the group. After discussing, students should record an answer based on the ideas and thoughts of the group.
16. Select a few groups to share their thoughts with the class and discuss.

Evidence of Understanding:

Collect the "Disaster Notes" (WS 1.5.1) to see that students completed each section and evaluated information they found.

Technology Integration:

Technology

NETS-S

6. Technology Operations and Concepts

Students demonstrate a sound understanding of technology concepts, systems, and operations. Students:

a. understand and use technology systems.
1. Instead of students recording their information on paper, use the "Disaster Notes Tech" (OEWS 1.5.1) option, in which students can record their information into a Word template.

Extension:

1. Read *Owen and Mzee: The True Story of a Remarkable Friendship* by Isabella Hatkoff (New York: Scholastic Press, 2006). This story will demonstrate one of the side

effects of natural disasters not often heard about—how natural disasters affect animals. This story will generate a lot of interest and discussion regarding natural disasters.

Suggested Modifications:

Students in need of modifications may find the underlined sections of the "Disaster Notes" (WS 1.5.1) worksheet more search friendly. Suggest that students locate the underlined information to better contribute to the group assignment.

DISASTER TOPIC LIST

Wildfire	Avalanche	Wildfire	Avalanche
Tornado	Tsunami	Tornado	Tsunami
Earthquake	Landslide	Earthquake	Landslide
Hurricane	Flood	Hurricane	Flood

DISASTER NOTES

Names: _____

Use this sheet to take notes about your natural disaster.

Our group is researching _____.

GENERAL INFORMATION

Questions to answer	Information found using online encyclopedia	Information found using Wikipedia	Information found in books
What are the causes of this natural disaster?			
When is this natural disaster most likely to occur?			
What kinds of damage occur as a result of this natural disaster?			
Is there a scale for measuring the intensity of your natural disaster? Explain how this scale works, the levels, etc.			
Can this natural disaster be predicted before it occurs? If so, how is this accomplished?			

AN EVENT IN HISTORY

Questions to answer	Information found using online encyclopedia	Information found using Wikipedia	Information found in books
Locate a specific time in history when your particular disaster occurred. Was there a name given? If so, what was it, and when and where did it occur?			
How many injuries/deaths were recorded?			
Describe any costs, damages, and or losses caused by this disaster.			

Source citations: _____

_____

_____

_____

Did you find any conflicting information in your research? Explain how you accepted or rejected this information. _____

_____

_____

Which source did you find to be more reliable? Why? _____

_____

_____

_____

5TH-GRADE LESSONS

LESSON 2: NEWSWORTHY EVENTS

Coordinate! This lesson uses the TFK (Time For Kids) Web site (http://www.timeforkids.com/TFK/) to demonstrate the proper way for students to write a news article. *Coordinate* with the classroom teacher by offering to share some news articles with the students and to demonstrate the proper way to write a news article. The classroom teacher may wish for the students to have extra writing practice.

Cooperate! Share the news stories created by the students with the classroom teacher. *Cooperate* by making a plan to broadcast the news stories over the morning announcements. Students can get practical public speaking practice. Offer to assist the classroom teacher in filming students performing their news story and share the videos with other classes or post it on your school Web site.

Lesson Plan

Integrated Goals:

Standard 8. Students use a variety of technological and information resources (e.g., libraries, databases, computer networks, video) to gather and synthesize information and to create and communicate knowledge.

Standard 12. Students use spoken, written, and visual language to accomplish their own purposes (e.g., for learning, enjoyment, persuasion, and the exchange of information).

Science in Personal and Social Perspectives

Content Standard F: Grades 5–8

As a result of activities in grades 5–8, all students should develop understanding of

• Natural hazards

Library Media

AASL 21st Century Standards

Standard 2: Draw conclusions, make informed decisions, apply knowledge to new situations, and create new knowledge.

Standard 3: Share knowledge and participate ethically and productively as members of our democratic society.

Essential Questions:

How does the use of multiple resources assist in completing more thorough research? When is it appropriate to use Wikipedia?

Desired Understandings:

Students will understand:

Why it is important to cross-check more than one resource when conducting research.
The differences between traditional encyclopedias and Wikipedia.
How to tell when a source is "reliable."

Integrated Objectives:

- Students will use online encyclopedias, Wikipedia, and books to research natural disasters and a natural disaster in history.
- Students will create a news story about a natural disaster in history.

Time Required:

45 minutes

Provided Materials:

- "Disaster Notes" (WS 1.5.1) completed from previous class
- "Disaster News" (WS 1.5.2)—one per student—printed back to back
- "Comparison Q's" (TRS 1.5.1)

Materials You Will Need to Obtain:

- Computer
- Projection device
- Pencils
- Computers for student use with access to World Book Online or another reliable online encyclopedia, and Wikipedia
- Access to articles about natural disasters
- Books about natural disasters

Prior to the Lesson

Prior to student arrival, locate an interesting piece of information currently being shared in the media to share with the class. This fact should be able to be confirmed by using the encyclopedia.

Lesson Procedures

Engagement:

1. Invite students sit in a circle. Join in the circle. Tell students that today they will participate in a game in which they will need to rely on their listening skills.
2. Whisper to the student to your right the information you heard about on the news and instruct them to whisper it to the person to their right, and so on, until the message comes back to you.
3. Share both the new statement as well as the original statement.
4. Explain to students that sometimes information can get twisted and misinterpreted once it is shared, and it is a good idea to go back to the original source and check for accuracy.

Activity:

5. Display a natural disaster news story from the Website Time for Kids (http://www.timeforkids.com/TFK/). Keep the article on display for use during the first activity.

6. Distribute copies of "Disaster News" (WS 1.5.2) to each student. Instruct students to look at the organizational side of the worksheet.

7. Explain that every good news article answers the questions *who, what, when, where, why,* and *how.*

8. Read the article aloud to the class, and ask for students to use their organizational sheet as a guide to help them remember each of the important parts of the story. Call on students to identify each of these important parts.

Transition:

9. Distribute copies of "Disaster Notes" (WS 1.5.1) back to the appropriate groups.

Activity:

10. Ask that students take the information they found in the previous class, and work with the other members of their group to organize the information into the appropriate categories of the "Disaster News" (WS 1.5.2) worksheet. Students may need access to the online encyclopedia and Wikipedia again to complete and confirm their research.

Embedded AASL Skills Indicator: ___.___.___: _____

_____

11. Give students time to complete the chart on the "Disaster News" (WS 1.5.2) worksheet.

Embedded AASL Skills Indicator: ___.___.___: _____

_____

Embedded AASL Dispositions in Action Indicator: ___.___.___: _____

_____

12. When students have completed the chart, ask that they work with the other members of their group to write a catchy and creative news story about their historic natural disaster into the news side of the "Disaster News" (WS 1.5.2) worksheet.

Embedded AASL Responsibilities Indicator: ___.___.___: _____

_____

13. Be sure and remind students that they are pretending this is a current news story even though it happened in the past, and that they should include the appropriate date.

Closure:

14. Ask students to read aloud their news stories to share with the class.

Embedded AASL Self-Assessment Strategies: ___.___.___: _____

_____

15. Use the "Comparison Q's" (TRS 1.5.1) to prompt a discussion with the class about online encyclopedias vs. Wikipedia.

Evidence of Understanding:

Collect and grade the "Disaster News" (WS 1.5.2) worksheet. Check that students were able to extract the necessary information from their research and compose a creative news story.

Enrichment Using Technology:

1. Have students record their "Disaster News" (WS 1.5.2) story into a podcast. Your podcast can be easily created using Audacity (http://audacity.sourceforge.net/) or by using an application you may already have available on your computer such as GarageBand.

Extension:

1. Have students brainstorm ideas about when an online encyclopedia or Wikipedia can and should be used for a project or to locate information. Students can use the "Which One?" (EX 1.5.1) worksheet to record their ideas. Students can then use the ideas from the worksheet to create a poster to display. The poster can be displayed in both the reference section and next to the computer to assist other students in choosing which encyclopedia resource to use.

Suggested Modifications:

For some students, it may be easier to verbally communicate their ideas. Use an audio recorder to have students communicate their news story.

DISASTER NEWS

Name: _____

Use this sheet to record the WWWWWH about the specific natural disaster in history that you chose to write about.

WWWWWH

Who? (or what disaster is this article about?)			
What? (What happened, or caused this disaster to happen?)			
When? (When did this disaster take place?)			
Where? (Where did this disaster take place?)			
Why? (Why is this an important disaster?			
How? (How did this disaster occur? How did it affect humans, animals, and the environment?)			

Write your own news story on the lines below. Use the information you recorded to write your own catchy and creative news story about your natural disaster. Tell your story from the perspective of a news anchor on a TV station, and pretend that it is the day the event occurred.

THIS JUST IN . . . DISASTER STRIKES!

_____

_____

_____

_____

_____

_____

_____

_____

_____

_____

_____

_____

_____

_____

_____

_____

_____

_____

_____

_____

_____

_____

_____

_____

COMPARISON Q'S

1. Which encyclopedia did you find easier to use—the online version or Wikipedia?

   _____

   _____

   _____

2. Which resource did you think contained more information about each subject? Explain your answer.

   _____

   _____

   _____

3. Which resource is more current? Explain.

   _____

   _____

   _____

4. What differences did you notice in the way each was structured?

   _____

   _____

   _____

5. Are there any tools available only in online encyclopedias or only in Wikipedia? What are they, and how are they used?

   _____

   _____

   _____

6. Which resource would you more likely use at home? At school? In the library? Why?

   _____

   _____

   _____

WHICH ONE?

Name: _____

Brainstorm some ideas of when it would be a good idea to use online encyclopedias and when it would be a good idea to use Wikipedia. Record your ideas below.

You should use ONLINE encyclopedias when . . .	**You should use WIKIPEDIA when . . .**
_____	_____
_____	_____
_____	_____
_____	_____
_____	_____
_____	_____
_____	_____
_____	_____
_____	_____
_____	_____
_____	_____
_____	_____
_____	_____
_____	_____
_____	_____
_____	_____
_____	_____
_____	_____

Working in Collaboration

Collaborate! True collaboration requires both the library media specialist and the classroom teacher to share in the design of integrated instruction. Collaboration provides you with an excellent opportunity to design inquiry-based learning activities. Here are some ideas for collaborating with the classroom teachers.

5th Grade: Science and Math

Essential Question: How do humans prepare for the risks of natural disasters?

- After conducting their research, students can create a comparison chart documenting the risks of various natural disasters and how these risks can be assessed. Students can use math concepts to graph and compare the risk factors of various natural disasters and share their findings in an informational session for parents, students, and staff.

For further information, please visit
www.destinationcollaboration.com

Bibliography
Works Cited

Dionysius525, S. *The Moon From Earth*. Photograph. 14 November. 2007. S. Dionysius525. 26 Sept. 2010. <http://commons.wikimedia.org/wiki/File:The_moon.jpg>.

Eisenberg, Michael B, and Robert E Berkowitz. *The Big6*. 1987. Web. 3 July 2008. <http://www.big6.com/>.

The Geometry of Earthshine. Diagram. NASA. 12 Apr. 2002. 28 Dec. 2008 <http://commons.wikimedia.org/wiki/File:Earthshine_diagram.png>.

Kazerounian, Kazem. "Robots." *World Book Online Reference Center*. 2008. Web. 25 May 2008 <http://www.worldbookonline.com/>.

Leonard, John. "Preservation Hall Applause." MP3. *SoundSnap*. Ed. Tasos Frantzolas. Web. 2 July 2008. <http://www.soundsnap.com/node/57024>.

McGinnis, Terri. "Cat." *World Book Online Reference Center*. World Book. Web. 2 July 2008. <http://www.worldbookonline.com/>.

McGinnis, Terri. "Rabbit." *World Book Online Reference Center*. World Book. Web. 2 July 2008. <http://www.worldbookonline.com/>.

Spudis, Paul D. "Moon." *World Book Online Reference Center*. World Book. Web. 17 May 2008. <http://www.worldbookonline.com/>.

Squyres, Steven, W. "Mars." *World Book Online Reference Center*. World Book. Web. 2 July 2008. <http://www.worldbookonline.com/>.

Winkvist, S. *LIDAR equipped Mobile Robot*. Photograph. 3 Mar. 2008. S. Winkvist. 28 Dec. 2008 <http://commons.wikimedia.org/wiki/File:LIDAR_equipped_mobile_robot.jpg>.

Suggested Book Resource

Hatkoff, Isabella, Craig Hatkoff, and Paula Kahumbu. *Owen and Mzee: The True Story of a Remarkable Friendship*. New York: Scholastic Press, 2006. Print.

Suggested Web Resources

Audacity Development Team, prod. *Audacity: Free Audio Editor and Recorder*. Sourceforge, 2010. Web. 3 Oct. 2010. <http://audacity.sourceforge.net/>.

"Discovery Streaming." Discovery Education. Discovery Communications, LLC, 2010. Web. 3 Oct. 2010. <http://streaming.discoveryeducation.com/>.

Encyclopedia Britannica Kids. Encyclopedia Britannica. 2010. Web. 7 Jan. 2010. <http://kids.britannica.com/>.

Fact Monster. Pearson Education, publishing as Fact Monster. 2009. Web. 7 Jan. 2010. <http://www.factmonster.com/>.

Time for Kids. Time Inc., 2008. Web. 29 Dec. 2008. <http://www.timeforkids.com/TFK/>.

"Video: Animals, Travel, Kids." *National Geographic*. National Geographic Society, 2010. Web. 3 Oct. 2010. <http://video.nationalgeographic.com/video/>.

"Welcome to Webkinz." *Webkinz*, GANZ, 2010. Web. 3 Oct. 2010. <http://www.webkinz.com>.

"Wikipedia, the Free Encyclopedia." *Wikipedia*. Wikimedia Foundation, Inc., 2010. Web. 3 Oct. 2010. <http://www.wikipedia.org/>.

Chapter 2

Atlases: Using Reference Tools

Introduction

The atlas is a tool that students should know how to use in order to pinpoint a location on a map, give or locate directions using coordinates, and gain knowledge and understanding about our changing world. The ability to locate this information is dependant upon knowledge of map terms and comfort level in using a map. To be effective users of the types of information that maps provide, students must be able to understand how to use indexes, coordinates, keys, legends, scales, and so forth. The two-lesson units for 3rd, 4th, and 5th grade will assist students in using atlases in both print and online formats.

From Year to Year

The atlas is a tool that will assist students in learning more about places in our world. The lessons in this chapter build on each other, so that by the end of 5th grade, all students will be aware of the vast differences of land features, climate, population, and economy in our world. The 3rd-grade lessons begin with map basics. Students will learn the differences between political and physical maps, map tools (scale, key/legend, and compass rose), and how to use an atlas's table of contents and index to find information. Students will create their own simple map and legend. In the 4th-grade lessons, students expand their map expertise to include climate, economy, population and precipitation maps. Students will define their perfect vacation spot by completing a questionnaire and share their results with a classmate. The classmate will become their travel agent and use the questionnaire and atlas to locate a destination that meets the student's criteria for a perfect vacation. The lessons for 5th grade extend students' knowledge of the atlas by introducing the concept of using coordinates, latitude, and longitude to locate places on a map. Students will interview family members to learn where their family originated and create a guessing game for classmates by providing clues and coordinates for the location. The atlas provides students with experiences in learning more about our Earth, the differences in climate, population, and economy and how these differences affect the lives of people.

Lifelong Library Use

This chapter provides students with the opportunity to connect to the real world and the larger community through the use of an atlas. Students are asked to collaborate and share information informally about maps and use map skills to learn more about different communities around the world. Learning how to locate places and find information in an atlas will assist students as they learn more about their place in the world and about in what ways their local environment is different from other environments. Acknowledging differences in places around the world is a first step toward an understanding and acceptance of cultural similarities and differences influenced by environment. Atlas use will provide students experience with a reference tool that can be used for a variety of purposes. Lifelong library users recognize the need for information and know how to use resources for a variety of purposes to locate information.

Self-Assessment Strategies

The atlas can be a difficult reference tool for students to understand and properly use. Much of the self-assessments provided in this chapter focus on students seeking help when it is needed and to recognize new knowledge and understanding. These strategies will assist students as they reflect on their learning. Students are asked to think about their own learning, assess the quality of their learning products, and provide feedback to one another throughout the learning process. Some lessons include rubrics for students' self-assessment use.

Relevancy

The Internet provides us with the ability to easily cross political, cultural, and geographic boundaries to communicate, work, and share intellectual resources. Elementary students' view of the world is often limited by their lack of life experience. Atlas use gives students a first look at the wide variety of places and people found in our world. Using atlases helps students learn how to determine their place in the world and view aspects of their local environment that they might not have thought about previously. Students must understand that what may be true for their own experience with climate, economic choices, and population may not be true everywhere in the world. Understanding these differences is essential as students begin to understand our complex world. Students will have the opportunity to use atlases in a variety of ways to locate and understand information through the use of maps and map tools.

Working in Isolation

Teaching students how to use the atlas will give them insights into reading maps and understanding geographic features, political boundaries, and a wide variety of regional statistics. Traditionally, atlases have been bound books found in reference sections of libraries, but there are now a wide variety atlases available in multimedia formats.

Classroom teachers may not know what types of atlases are available in your library media center. Look them over and think about how the atlases you have support curriculum goals in your school. If you have special atlases covering a distinctive topic, be sure to share them with your classroom teachers.

If your school hosts a geography bee, discuss with the social studies coordinator how you can assist with the instructional needs of the students. It is important to remember that reading maps can facilitate high-order thinking skills, such as inferring how an environment can affect culture. As you design lessons for atlas use, think about how using an atlas could facilitate students with comparing different ecosystems and climates; exploring your state; and using maps in conjunction with learning about current events. As you begin to share your ideas and resources, you will be seen as an instructional leader in your school.

3RD-GRADE LESSONS

LESSON 1: AROUND THE WORLD

Coordinate! This atlas lesson gives students an introduction to basic map tools and features, including information about when it is best to use a map as opposed to a globe. *Coordinate* with the classroom teacher and teach this lesson when students are beginning to use maps in the classroom.

Cooperate! After students have completed "Cartographer Kids" (WS 2.3.1), share these with the classroom teacher. *Coordinate* with the classroom teacher to see when students will be learning about their own state or region. Offer to locate a blank map of your area for students to then study and add in their own physical features and landmarks.

Lesson Plan

Integrated Goals:

Language Arts

Standard 8. Students use a variety of technological and information resources (e.g., libraries, databases, computer networks, video) to gather and synthesize information and to create and communicate knowledge.

Social Studies

III People, Places, & Environments

a. construct and use mental maps of locales, regions, and the world that demonstrate understanding of relative location, direction, size, and shape.

Library Media

AASL 21st Century Standards

Standard 1: Inquire, think critically, and gain knowledge.

Essential Questions:

How can map tools help you locate information in an atlas in order to answer an information need?

Desired Understandings:

Students will understand:

How to use map tools to locate information in an atlas.
How to determine different types of maps in an atlas.

Integrated Objectives:

- Students will learn basic map and atlas skills.
- Students will create a map using the skills they learned.

Time Required:

45 minutes

Provided Materials:

- "Map Basics" (OER 2.3.1) PowerPoint
- "Cartographer Kids" (WS 2.3.1)—one per student

Materials You Will Need to Obtain:

- Globe
- Medium-sized tote bag
- Road atlas
- Colored pencils and/or crayons
- A class set of atlases
- Projection device
- Pencils
- Computer

Lesson Procedures:

Engagement:

1. When students enter the room, tell them that you will be with them in just a minute. Proceed to attempt to fit a globe into a tote bag. Use exaggerated moves as you try to squeeze the globe into the tote bag. Explain that after school you are going to take a trip to a mall that you have never been to before and are going to use the globe to figure out how to get there from school. Ask students if they think it is a good idea for you to use the globe for directions.

Activity:

2. Ask students to explain why a globe is or is not a good tool to use for directions. Ask for students to give examples of good tools to use to figure out directions from the school to the mall. Answers could include: road atlas, navigation system, Google Maps, or Mapquest.
3. Display the "Map Basics" (OER 2.3.1) PowerPoint.
4. Distribute atlases to the class and instruct students to use their atlases to follow along with the "Map Basics" (OER 2.3.1) PowerPoint.
5. Follow the directions in the notes portion of the "Map Basics" (OER 2.3.1) Power-Point.

Embedded AASL Responsibilities Indicator: ___.___.___: _____

_____

6. Ask students to locate the parts of the map in their atlases as you discuss and display them in the "Map Basics" (OER 2.3.1) PowerPoint.

Transition:

7. Distribute copies of "Cartographer Kids" (WS 2.3.1).

Activity:

8. Explain the directions to students.

Embedded AASL Skills Indicator: ___.___.___: _____

_____

Embedded AASL Dispositions in Action Indicator: ___.___.___: _____

_____

9. Allow students time to complete the "Cartographer Kids" (WS 2.3.1) worksheet. Tell students to use the atlases at their table to assist them in creating their map.

Embedded AASL Self-Assessment Strategies: ___.___.___: _____

_____

10. Instruct students to ask for help when needed.

Closure:

11. Ask students to share some of the symbols they chose to use for their map and why they chose them.

Evidence of Understanding:

Collect and grade "Cartographer Kids" (WS 2.3.1), checking that students were successful in their use of map symbols.

Technology Integration:

Technology

NETS-S

6. Technology Operations and Concepts

Students demonstrate a sound understanding of technology concepts, systems, and operations. Students:

CLASSROOM CONNECTIONS

Provide classroom teachers with a list of "Think Abouts" that explain how to integrate atlas use in the classroom. Offer to collaborate to develop lessons that integrate content and information literacy objectives.

a. understand and use technology systems.

Instead of using the traditional "Cartographer Kids" (WS 2.3.1) worksheet, use the "Cartographer Kids Tech" (OEWS 2.3.1) worksheet on a computer. Students will need to use draw tools in Word to add rivers, lakes, boxes, and so forth, on their key.

Extension:

1. Read the book *Me on the Map* by Joan Sweeney (New York: Crown, 1996) and use the examples in the story as a reinforcement for the lesson activities.

Suggested Modifications:

For students in need of modifications, instruct these students to create only three symbols for their map on the "Cartographer Kids" (WS 2.3.1) worksheet. Try to pair students with reading difficulties with stronger readers when sharing the "Map Basics" (OER 2.3.1) PowerPoint.

CARTOGRAPHER KIDS

Name: _____

Directions: Use the United States outline below to create your own map. Add your own features and symbols and then use the map key below to show what each symbol andcolor means. You should have at least five symbols in your key. Use colored pencils or crayons to add color to your map.

Map Title: _____

Map Key

Blank Map of the United States. Map. *Wikimedia*. 2 Dec. 2007. Web. 4 Oct. 2008. ‹http://commons.wikimedia.org/wiki/Image:Blank_map_of_the_United_States.PNG›.

3RD-GRADE LESSONS

LESSON 2: A-T-L-A-S

Coordinate! Students review what they know about atlases and gain new knowledge by playing an "Atlas Bingo" (OMN 2.3.1) game. Students record what else they wish to know about atlases and how to use them. *Coordinate* with the classroom teacher by sharing the "What Have I Learned?" (WS 2.3.2) self-assessment sheet to show what students have an interest in learning more about. The classroom teacher can use these comments when planning their lessons incorporating the use of maps.

Cooperate! Students will enjoy playing the educational "Atlas Bingo" (OMN 2.3.1) game in library media class. *Cooperate* with the classroom teacher by offering to share the bingo game cards. The classroom teacher may enjoy using this game as a station in the classroom or as a follow-up activity when using atlases in the classroom.

Lesson Plan

Integrated Goals:

Language Arts

Standard 8. Students use a variety of technological and information resources (e.g., libraries, databases, computer networks, video) to gather and synthesize information and to create and communicate knowledge.

Social Studies

III People, Places, & Environments

a. construct and use mental maps of locales, regions, and the world that demonstrate understanding of relative location, direction, size, and shape.

Library Media

AASL 21st Century Standards

  Standard 1: Inquire, think critically, and gain knowledge.

Essential Questions:

  How can map tools help you locate information in an atlas in order to answer an information need?
  What can maps help you to accomplish in everyday life?

Desired Understandings:

Students will understand:

How to use map tools to locate information in an atlas.
How to use maps in everyday situations.

Integrated Objectives:

- Students will participate in a bingo game to recall and review terms in an atlas.
- Students will review what they learned and will determine what else they would like to learn about atlases.

Time Required:

45 minutes

Provided Materials:

- "Atlas Song" (RS 2.3.1)
- "Atlas Bingo" (OMN 2.3.1)—one bingo card per student (print on cardstock and laminate to use from year to year)
- "Bingo Questions" (OER 2.3.3) PowerPoint
- "Bingo Answers" (OER 2.3.4) PowerPoint
- "What Have I Learned?" (WS 2.3.2)—one per student

Materials You Will Need to Obtain:

- Scrap paper, or small items such as dry beans or seashells to be used for bingo markers
- Classroom set of atlases
- Computer
- Projection device
- Pencils

Optional Materials:

- Bookmarks, stickers, maps, or small prizes for the bingo winners if desired.

Lesson Procedures:

Engagement:

1. Display and sing the "Atlas Song" (RS 2.3.1) to students. Students may sing along if they wish.
2. After the song is finished, see if students can recall some of the facts mentioned in the song.

Activity:

Embedded AASL Skills Indicator: ___.___.___: _____

_____

3. Explain to students that today they will be playing an atlas bingo game to review basic atlas skills. Most of the answers to the bingo questions can be found in the atlas.
4. Distribute an "Atlas Bingo" (OMN 2.3.1) card to each student, along with a set of bingo markers.

5. Ask students to look at their "Atlas Bingo" (OMN 2.3.1) cards. Point out that each card is different, and not all the cards contain the same terms.

Embedded AASL Dispositions in Action Indicator: ___.___.___: _____

_____

Embedded AASL Skills Indicator: ___.___.___: _____

_____

6. Explain that you will select questions to read aloud to the class. Students should listen carefully to the question and work with members sitting at their table to come up with an answer using the available atlases. Once the table has come to an agreement on the answer, they can use a bingo marker to place over the correct word on their "Atlas Bingo" (OMN 2.3.1) card (if they have the word).
7. After giving students time to answer the question, ask for a team to volunteer the answer. Make sure the correct answer is clear to the class before proceeding to the next question. Continue asking questions until someone receives "bingo." Determine how bingo will be achieved prior to beginning the game (e.g., four corners, railroad tracks, box, five in a row, etc.).
8. Check to make sure the student has a good bingo. If the student does not, continue game play until there is a winner. Once bingo has been achieved, play the game again several times with the class until students have gained a clear understanding for the material.

Transition:

9. After playing several "Atlas Bingo" (OMN 2.3.1) games with the students, have students clear their cards and neatly stack the bingo cards.
10. Distribute "What Have I Learned?" (WS 2.3.2).

Activity:

Embedded AASL Responsibilities Indicator: ___.___.___: _____

_____

Embedded AASL Self-Assessment Strategies: ___.___.___: _____

_____

11. Read each question aloud to students.
12. Give students time to complete "What Have I Learned?" (WS 2.3.2).

Closure:

13. Have students share their answers from "What Have I Learned?" (WS 2.3.2). If students have answered that they need clarification on a particular term or more

assistance regarding the use of atlases, clarify and provide extra practice for the student.

14. Collect "What Have I Learned?" (WS 2.3.2).

Evidence of Understanding:

Observe students as they work together to locate information in the atlas. Review as necessary by playing the "Atlas Bingo" (OMN 2.3.1) game again until students are comfortable with using atlases. Check "What Have I Learned?" (WS 2.3.2) to make sure students have gained an understanding for how to use atlases.

Enrichment Using Technology:

Allow students time to explore National Geographic's "Map Machine" (http://ngm.national geographic.com/map-machine#theme=Street&c=0|0&sf=187648892.534865).

Discuss the types of maps available on the Web site. Discuss if students find them easier or more difficult to use than a print atlas.

Extension:

1. Distribute copies of "My Own Country" (EX 2.3.1). Allow students time to complete the worksheets. Share together as a class.

Suggested Modifications:

Use the "Bingo Questions" (OER 2.3.3) PowerPoint to display the questions for those students in need of a visual aid.

ATLAS SONG

Directions: Sing song to the tune of "Bingo."

There was a god who held the world, right up on his shoulders

A-T-L-A-S,

A-T-L-A-S,

A-T-L-A-S

and Atlas was his name-o.

Ptolemy made the first map book around the year 100!

A-T-L-A-S,

A-T-L-A-S,

A-T-L-A-S

and Atlas was it's name-o.

Ortelius made a map book in 1570

A-T-L-A-S,

A-T-L-A-S,

A-T-L-A-S

and Atlas was it's name-o.

A few years later, Mercator gave the book a name-o

A-T-L-A-S,

A-T-L-A-S,

A-T-L-A-S

and he named it Atlas!

Ever since the 16th century, we have a name for map books!

A-T-L-A-S, A-T-L-A-S, A-T-L-A-S, and that is what we call them!

WHAT HAVE I LEARNED?

Name: _____

Directions: Answer each question below to reflect on what you have learned and to determine what you would like to learn in the future about maps and atlases.

1. What is one new thing you learned about maps and/or atlases?

   _____

   _____

   _____

2. Does what you learned change the way you will look for/use information in an atlas? How?

   _____

   _____

   _____

3. For what purpose can you use maps/atlases in the future?

   _____

   _____

   _____

4. Are there any words or features about maps and atlases that you don't understand and may need additional practice in understanding?

   _____

   _____

   _____

5. When exploring the atlas for today's activity, was there a particular part of the atlas that made you curious to know more? If so, which part, and what do you want to know more about?

   _____

   _____

   _____

MY OWN COUNTRY

Name: _____

Directions: Use the space below to create your own map. Add your own features and symbols and then use the map key below to show what each symbol/ color means. Explain on which continent your new country will be located. Be sure to include facts about your country. Use colored pencils or crayons to add color to your map.

Country Fast Facts
Capital:
Language: Country Flag:
Population:

Map Key

Working in Collaboration

Collaborate! True collaboration requires both the library media specialist and the classroom teacher to share in the design of integrated instruction. Collaboration provides you with an excellent opportunity to design inquiry-based learning activities. Here are some ideas for collaborating with the classroom teachers.

3rd Grade: Social Studies

Essential Question: How can atlases change the way I see the world?

- Have students create a new country or state. Expand the project to include having them create a physical, political, economic, population, or other statistical map of their choice for their new place. Ask students to compare their new country or state to a country or state already in existence that has the same or similar characteristics. Were their fantasy choices similar to reality? Why or why not?

> For further information, please visit
> www.destinationcollaboration.com

4TH-GRADE LESSONS

LESSON 1: GETTING TO KNOW THE WORLD

Coordinate! Students learn the various types of maps found in an atlas. They will become "experts" at discerning the differences and special attributes of a specific kind of map and share their findings with the class. In preparation of becoming and working with a travel agent, students will take a "Vacation Questionnaire" (WS 2.4.1) to determine where they would like to go on vacation. *Coordinate* with the classroom teacher by sharing the completed "Vacation Questionnaire" (WS 2.4.1) worksheets. The classroom teacher may wish to use them to better know their learners.

Cooperate! *Cooperate* with the classroom teacher by sharing which students became "experts" on a particular kind of map. The classroom teacher may use this information to better prepare instruction. Explain your lesson and the use of the "Vacation Questionnaire" (WS 2.4.1) to the classroom teacher. The classroom teacher may wish to extend your lesson by creating a project based on these introductory lessons.

Lesson Plan

Integrated Goals:

Language Arts

Standard 8. Students use a variety of technological and information resources (e.g., libraries, databases, computer networks, video) to gather and synthesize information and to create and communicate knowledge.

Social Studies

III People, Places, & Environments

b. interpret, use, and distinguish various representations of the earth, such as maps, globes, and photographs.

Library Media

AASL 21st Century Standards

Standard 1: Inquire, think critically, and gain knowledge.

Essential Questions:

How can different types of maps in an atlas assist in locating information?

Desired Understandings:

Students will understand:

How to use different types of maps to locate information in an atlas.

How to determine different types of maps in an atlas.

Integrated Objectives:

- Students will learn how to use an atlas and will understand its purpose.
- Students will become familiar with different types of maps found in an atlas and understand the purpose and function of these maps.

Time Required:

45 minutes

Provided Materials:

- "Vacation Questionnaire" (WS 2.4.1)—one per student
- "Many Maps" (OER 2.4.1) PowerPoint
- "Expert Cards" (MN 2.4.1)—one card per student

Materials You Will Need to Obtain:

- A set of atlases
- Computer
- Projection device
- Pencils
- Suitcase with beach items (e.g., beach ball, snorkel, towel, swimsuit, etc.)

Lesson Procedures:

Engagement:

1. Enter the room carrying a suitcase filled with beach items. Tell students that you always keep a suitcase packed just in case you have the opportunity to go to one of your favorite vacation spots. Begin unpacking the suitcase to show students the contents of the suitcase. Ask students to guess where you like to go on vacation.

Activity:

2. After students guess that you like to vacation at the beach, explain to them that they will be able to explore possible vacation spots for themselves using a tool called an atlas.
3. Display the "Many Maps" (OER 2.4.1) PowerPoint. Take the time to discuss the attributes of each type of map. Students may follow along in their own atlas at their table.
4. After showing and discussing the "Many Maps" (OER 2.4.1) PowerPoint, tell students that they will be travel agents and will have the opportunity to help their classmates choose the perfect vacation spot. Clarify for students the job description of a travel agent.

5. Distribute copies of "Vacation Questionnaire" (WS 2.4.1) to each student. Tell students they should complete the questionnaire in order to assist their travel agent in selecting the perfect vacation spot for their next trip.

Embedded AASL Skills Indicator: ___.___.___: _____

_____

6. Allow students time to complete the "Vacation Questionnaire" (WS 2.4.1).
7. Collect the "Vacation Questionnaire" (WS 2.4.1) from each student and set aside for later redistribution.
8. Explain to students that they will need to become experts in their field. In order to accomplish this, they will be assigned a particular type of map to look at and determine why it might be important for a travel agent to have this kind of map.

Transition:

9. Distribute the "Expert Cards" (MN 2.4.1) to students. Tell students that they should get in a group with other "travel agents" with the same expert card.
10. Allow students time to put themselves into groups.

Activity:

Embedded AASL Responsibilities Indicator: ___.___.___: _____

_____

11. Explain that students will become experts on the type of map they have on their "Expert Card" (MN 2.4.1). With their teammates, students should collaborate to determine the type of map they have been assigned, its function, and how and when it should be used.
12. Discuss how to use an atlas's table of contents and index to assist in finding the proper map.
13. Allow students time to collaborate with their teammates to formulate a brief oral report.

Embedded AASL Dispositions in Action Indicator: ___.___.___: _____

_____

14. Ask each team to give a brief oral report on their findings to the class.
15. Explain to students that they are going to be using each of the maps in an atlas in order to be a travel agent and find the perfect vacation spot for their classmate.
16. Point out to students that each question on the "Vacation Questionnaire" (WS 2.4.1) aligns with a map in the atlas (also explain which map aligns with each question).

17. Display the "Many Maps" (OER 2.4.1) PowerPoint again to demonstrate how to use each of the featured maps to locate appropriate vacation spots.

Closure:

Embedded AASL Self-Assessment Strategies: ___.___.___: _____

_____

18. As you dismiss the class, ask students to name and explain different kinds of maps can be found in atlases.

Evidence of Understanding:

As students work in groups to become experts for their particular map, assess their ability to work together and explain their map's features.

Enrichment Using Technology:

Have your students visit the National Atlas Web site, http://www.nationalatlas.gov/natlas/Natlasstart.asp. Give them time to explore and create their own map with various special features.

Extension:

Ask students to find an article about a current event in a newspaper, magazine, or Time magazine's Time For Kids Web site (http://www.timeforkids.com/TFK/). Then, have students locate a map in the atlas that correlates with the article they picked. For example, if students find an article about the Olympics in Vancouver, they could locate a map of Vancouver, Canada, in their atlas. Students could look at the physical features of the area as well as bordering countries in order to make better connections to current events.

Suggested Modifications:

Students with difficulties in regards to using maps should be paired with students who are competent in using maps.

VACATION QUESTIONNAIRE

Customer name:_____

1. Look at the list below. Select your three favorite land features. Place a "1" next your first choice, a "2" next to your second choice, and a "3" next to your third choice.

_____ Lake   _____ Mountain   _____ River

_____ Desert   _____ Ocean   _____ Forest

_____ Island   _____ Glacier   _____ Swamp

To be completed by travel agent. I will use the _____ map.

2. Look at the list of climates below. Select your top two. Place a "1" next to your first choice, a "2" next to your second choice

_____ Arid   _____ Mediterranean   _____ Polar

(Dry, lack of water)   (Hot, dry summers and cool, wet winters)   (Frozen, icy, and snowy)

_____ Tropical   _____ Continental

(Temperature is always summery)   (Cold winters, warm and rainy above 64°F)

To be completed by travel agent. I will use the _____ map.

3. Check one. Would you prefer to be near a

_____ Capital city   _____ Major city   _____ Small town

To be completed by travel agent. I will use the _____ map.

4. What activities do you enjoy? Check all that apply.

☐ Biking   ☐ Hiking   ☐ Swimming   ☐ Skiing

☐ Snorkeling   ☐ Climbing   ☐ Sailing   ☐ Sun Bathing

☐ Reading   ☐ Sightseeing   ☐ Golf   ☐ Tennis

☐ Other Sports _____   ☐ Other _____

To be completed by travel agent. Vacation location: _____ Travel agent's signature: _____

EXPERT CARDS

Political	Physical
Climate	**Economy**
Population	**Elevation**

4TH-GRADE LESSONS

LESSON 2: PLANNING A TRIP

 **Coordinate!** Students will become a travel agent in order to find the perfect vacation spot for a classmate based on the responses of their classmates' "Vacation Questionnaire" (WS 2.4.1). Students will use political, physical, and climate maps in order to decide where to send their customer. Consider *coordinating* with the classroom teacher to use this lesson by integrating math skills to create a vacation budget.

Cooperate! After teaching this lesson, *cooperate* with the classroom teacher by offering to demonstrate how to use Google Earth, if necessary. The classroom teacher may wish to extend the project by asking students to research their country and share their findings in a Google Earth presentation.

Lesson Plan

Integrated Goals:

Language Arts

Standard 8. Students use a variety of technological and information resources (e.g., libraries, databases, computer networks, video) to gather and synthesize information and to create and communicate knowledge.

Standard 12. Students use spoken, written, and visual language to accomplish their own purposes (e.g., for learning, enjoyment, persuasion, and the exchange of information).

Social Studies

III People, Places, & Environments

b. interpret, use, and distinguish various representations of the earth, such as maps, globes, and photographs.

Library Media

AASL 21st Century Standards

   Standard 1: Inquire, think critically, and gain knowledge.

Essential Questions:

   How can maps provide the end user with a variety of information about different places around the world?

Desired Understandings:

Students will understand:

How to use different types of maps to locate information in an atlas.

How to determine different types of maps in an atlas.

Integrated Objectives:

- Students will use the various maps in an atlas to select the perfect vacation destination for a classmate.

Time Required:

45 minutes

Provided Materials:

- "Vacation Questionnaire" (WS 2.4.1)—completed from the previous lesson
- "Pack a Suitcase" (WS 2.4.2)—one per student
- "Sample Vacation Questionnaire" (RS 2.4.1)

Materials You Will Need to Obtain:

- A set of atlases
- Computer
- Projection device
- Pencils

Prior to the Lesson:

Select 20–30 books about various places around the world. Set these on display in the instructional area of your media center, next to a map of the world. Display the books according to continent to assist students in locating a book about their destination later in the class.

Lesson Procedures:

Engagement:

1. Direct the student's attention to the display books from around the world. Tell students that although the media center has a wide variety of books on countries, not every country is represented. Explain to students that today their travel agent will select a place for them to go on their perfect vacation. Ask students to volunteer what they believe a travel agent does.

Activity:

2. Randomly redistribute the "Vacation Questionnaire" (WS 2.4.1) completed in the previous lesson, as well as an atlas for each student. Ensure that students do not receive back their own questionnaire.

3. Explain to students that the student who's "Vacation Questionnaire" (WS 2.4.1) they have in their hand will now be their customer. The students will be travel agents for their customer.

4. Display the "Sample Vacation Questionnaire" (RS 2.4.1). Point out the boxes on the questionnaire that need to be filled out by the travel agent (the student who

now has the "Vacation Questionnaire" [WS 2.4.1] in their possession). Discuss with students the proper map that should be used for each question to locate the perfect vacation spot for the customer.

5. Allow students time to write each type of map in the spaces provided on the "Vacation Questionnaire" (RS 2.4.1) for later reference.

Embedded AASL Skills Indicator: ___.___.___: _____

_____

6. With the "Sample Vacation Questionnaire" (RS 2.4.1) on display, model for students your thinking as if you were the travel agent for this fictional customer. Show students in the atlas where you would send this customer on vacation based on their answers from the questionnaire (Madagascar could be one of many possibilities). Be sure and point out all the reasons why this is the perfect vacation spot for this customer.

Embedded AASL Responsibilities Indicator: ___.___.___: _____

_____

7. Give students time to locate the perfect vacation spot for their customer. They should then write the location, along with their signature at the bottom of the "Vacation Questionnaire" (RS 2.4.1). While students should try their best to locate a vacation spot that has most of the customers' desires, they should at least locate a spot that has one of each of their requirements. Students may wish to circle the areas of the "Vacation Questionnaire" (RS 2.4.1) on which they will focus.

8. Display the "Pack a Suitcase" (WS 2.4.2) worksheet. Demonstrate to students how it should be completed.

9. Distribute the "Pack a Suitcase" (WS 2.4.2) worksheet to each student.

Embedded AASL Skills Indicator: ___.___.___: _____

_____

10. Allow students time to complete the worksheet. Upon completion of the worksheet, students can give the "Pack a Suitcase" (WS 2.4.2) worksheet to the "customer" to whom they were assigned.

Closure:

Embedded AASL Self-Assessment Strategies: ___.___.___: _____

_____

11. Once students have given their customer their "Pack a Suitcase" (WS 2.4.2) worksheet explaining the vacation they have selected for them, students should wait for feedback from the customer, explaining whether the vacation selected was one they think they would enjoy.

Embedded AASL Dispositions in Action Indicator: ___.___.___: _____

_____

12. Direct student's attention back to the book display at the front of the room. Explain that even though students may not be able to take the vacation of their choosing at this moment, they can take an armchair adventure (students can sit, read, and imagine about their vacation right from the comfort of their own chair) to a location at or near their vacation destination. Encourage students to check out any of the books on display, and assist students in locating a book in the non-fiction section of the media center if their vacation location is not on display.

Evidence of Understanding:

Check for student participation throughout the lesson.

Collect the "Pack a Suitcase" (WS 2.4.2) and "Vacation Questionnaire" (WS 2.4.1) worksheets. Check for completion of the worksheets and to see that students were successful in locating an appropriate vacation location for their customers.

Enrichment Using Technology:

1. Allow students to go to the Weather Channel's vacation and travel planner page, http://www.weather.com/activities/travel/vacationplanner/?from=secondarynav. There they will find all sorts of relevant and current information about various travel destinations including current weather forecasts, suggested travel dates, activities, and much more. Encourage students to look up their perfect destination to learn more.

2. If there is time, have students photograph one another using a digital camera. Download and resize the pictures, print them, and allow students to add their own photograph to the "Pack a Suitcase" (WS 2.4.2) worksheet they completed for their customer.

Extension:

1. Encourage students to be creative writers. Distribute "My Travel Journal" (EX 2.4.1) and give students the opportunity to describe the events that occur during their vacation to their perfect destination. Students will need access to more information about their vacation destination to know more about what they can expect when visiting.

Suggested Modifications:

This activity may be challenging for students with special needs. Allow students additional time to complete the activity.

PACK A SUITCASE

Customer name

Your next vacation destination is _____ , _____
(Country)   (Continent)

Land features in this country include _____

The climate is mostly _____
You may wish to stay in the city of _____ so that you will be close to _____

For your convenience, I have placed a red "x" on this map to indicate your vacation destination!

http://commons.wikimedia.org/wiki/Image:World_Map_Blank.svg accessed on 9.14.08

Travel Agent

Recommended method of transportation: _____

Recommended travel month: _____

Please let me know the next time you wish to book a vacation, I'll be more than happy to assist you!

Your Picture Here

Name of travel agent

In order to be prepared for your vacation, I've suggested a list of items you should bring and given reasons why they are necessary.

_____
_____
_____
_____
_____
_____
_____
_____
_____
_____
_____
_____
_____

SAMPLE VACATION QUESTIONNAIRE

Customer name:_____

1. Look at the list below. Select your three favorite land features. Place a "1" next your first choice, a "2" next to your second choice, and a "3" next to your third choice.

_____ Lake	__3__ Mountain	_____ River
_____ Desert	__1__ Ocean	_____ Forest
__2__ Island	_____ Glacier	_____ Swamp

To be completed by travel agent. I will use the _____ map.

2. Look at the list of climates below. Select your top two. Place a "1" next to your first choice, a "2" next to your second choice

_____ Arid	__2__ Mediterranean	_____ Polar
(Dry, lack of water)	(Hot, dry summers and cool, wet winters)	(Frozen, icy, and snowy)
__1__ Tropical	_____ Continental	
(Temperature is always summery)	(Cold winters, warm and rainy above 64°F)	

To be completed by travel agent. I will use the _____ map.

3. Check one. Would you prefer to be near a

_____ Capital city	__X__ Major city	_____ Small town

To be completed by travel agent. I will use the _____ map.

4. What activities do you enjoy? Check all that apply.

☐ Biking	☐ Hiking	■ Swimming	☐ Skiing
■ Snorkeling	☐ Climbing	☐ Sailing	☐ Sun Bathing
■ Reading	■ Sightseeing	☐ Golf	☐ Tennis
☐ Other Sports _____		☐ Other _____	

To be completed by travel agent.
Vacation location: _____
Travel agent's signature: _____

From *Destination Collaboration 2: A Complete Reference Focused Curriculum Guidebook to Educate 21st Century Learners in Grades 3–5* by Danielle N. DuPuis and Lori M. Carter. Santa Barbara, CA: Libraries Unlimited. Copyright © 2011.

MY TRAVEL JOURNAL

Dear Journal,   Date: _____

Today I _____

_____

_____

_____

_____

_____

_____

_____

_____

_____

_____

_____

_____

_____

_____

_____

_____

_____

_____

_____

_____

_____

_____

_____

Sincerely,

_____

Working in Collaboration

Collaborate! True collaboration requires both the library media specialist and the classroom teacher to share in the design of integrated instruction. Collaboration provides you with an excellent opportunity to design inquiry-based learning activities. Here are some ideas for collaborating with the classroom teachers.

4th Grade: Social Studies

Essential Question: How do different representations of the earth help us to better understand our changing planet?

- Use Google Maps for students to locate a place and then have them look at the various features such as terrain, satellite, traffic, and so forth. Students can create a PowerPoint presentation explaining how each type of map changed their perspective of an area.

4th Grade: Language Arts/Social Studies

Essential Question: How can maps help us to gain a deeper understanding of literature?

- Use Google Earth to design a "trip" based on a book read in the classroom. Students can locate and save places in Google Earth and then add in their own content (pictures, Web links, text, etc.) to make the experience more authentic and enjoyable. Examples on how to do this can be found at Google Lit Trips (www.googlelittrips.org).

For further information, please visit
www.destinationcollaboration.com

5TH-GRADE LESSONS

LESSON 1: POSTCARDS FROM PEDRO

Coordinate! Students receive a postcard from Pedro. Pedro gives the students hints about his location and the coordinates. Students are challenged to find his location using coordinates and the atlas. Students practice their skills by playing the "Matching Coordinates" (RS 2.5.2) game to pinpoint locations in the atlas. For homework, students are asked to interview their parents/guardians about where their family originated (This location may be another country or another state). *Coordinate* with the classroom teacher by sharing the homework assigned to students. The classroom teacher can help remind the students to take home and complete their homework.

Cooperate! Consider sharing the "My Family" (WS 2.5.2) worksheet with the classroom teacher. Explain that students will be asked to interview their parents/guardians about where their family originated. Be sensitive to the needs of the students: students may interview a classmate or the teacher if they do not have their own family to interview. Ask if this kind of interview is needed in the reading/language arts or social studies curriculum. *Coordinate* with the classroom teacher by offering to teach this lesson at the same time as students are learning how to conduct an interview during classroom instruction.

Lesson Plan

Integrated Goals:

Language Arts

Standard 12. Students use spoken, written, and visual language to accomplish their own purposes (e.g., for learning, enjoyment, persuasion, and the exchange of information).

Social Studies

III People, Places, & Environments

c. use appropriate resources, data sources, and geographic tools such as atlases, databases, grid systems, charts, graphs, and maps to generate, manipulate, and interpret information.

Library Media

AASL 21st Century Standards

Standard 1: Inquire, think critically, and gain knowledge.
Standard 2: Draw conclusions, make informed decisions, apply knowledge to new situations, and create new knowledge.

Essential Questions:

How can atlases provide the end user with a variety of information about different places around the world?

How do coordinates assist you when looking for a place on a map?

Desired Understandings:

Students will understand:

How to use different types of maps to locate information in an atlas.

How to determine when to use different types of maps in an atlas.

How to use coordinates to locate places in an atlas.

Integrated Objectives:

- Students will practice locating places in an atlas by using the index, coordinates, and place names.

Time Required:

45 minutes

Provided Materials:

- "Pedro's Postcard" (RS 2.5.1)—Prior to printing, type or write in your name and school address into the address label. Affix a stamp for a more authentic look.
- "Postcard Template" (WS 2.5.1)
- "Matching Coordinates" (RS 2.5.2)—Make enough copies for each pair of students to share. Laminate the cards if desired to make them last longer.
- "Matching Coordinates Answer Key" (TRS 2.5.1)
- "My Family" (WS 2.5.2)—one half sheet per student

Materials You Will Need to Obtain:

- Computer
- Projection device
- Pencils
- Class set of atlases
- Wall-sized world map

Lesson Procedures:

Engagement:

1. Tell students that a friend Pedro lives in Mexico. He's recently sent a postcard giving a description of where he lives, along with coordinates so that the students can locate his town on a map. Display and share "Pedro's Postcard" (RS 2.5.1) with the class.

Activity:

2. Ask students to recall the ways to navigate an atlas. Review how to use the index, and explain how to use coordinates.
3. Using the coordinates and clues Pedro has given, ask students to use their atlases to see if they can find Pedro's location on a map.

Embedded AASL Skills Indicator: ___.___.___ : _____

_____

4. Have students share their findings with the class (Pedro's location is Tabasco, Mexico). Ask students to share how they used the clues to infer and confirm Pedro's location. Discuss the best type of map to locate Pedro's location (Political Map) and why it was the most helpful/appropriate for this activity.

Transition:

5. Tell students that as a class, they will be writing a postcard to Pedro providing him clues about where they live and will also provide the coordinates of their location just as Pedro has done.

Activity:

Embedded AASL Responsibilities Indicator: ___.___.___ : _____

_____

6. Brainstorm clues with the class about the local area and jot down the ideas on the board. Some examples could include a major landmark close to the school or area, a major physical feature such as a lake or river, or even a state symbol. Have students determine the most appropriate maps to use for locating this information.

7. After brainstorming, have students look in their atlases to see if they can locate on a map where they live.

Embedded AASL Skills Indicator: ___.___.___ : _____

_____

8. Demonstrate for students how to use the longitude and latitude coordinates to locate a specific place on a map. Write the coordinates on the board. Ask students to look at their atlas to see if there are any other clues they could add to the list.

9. Together with the class, have students help you write a postcard to Pedro. You can either do this as a class, and write on the "Postcard Template" (WS 2.5.1) as it is displayed for the class, or you may choose to have each student write a postcard using their own words and a few of the clues you brainstormed together.

Transition:

10. Tell students how excited Pedro will be to get their postcard. Suggest to students that they should practice using coordinates in an atlas to prepare for the next class.

Activity:

11. Distribute the "Matching Coordinates" (RS 2.5.2) game to each pair of students.
12. Tell students that they should work with a partner and use the atlas to match up the coordinates with the correct place names. Remind students that they will need to use the index in order to locate the various places on a map.

Embedded AASL Dispositions in Action Indicator: ___.___.___: _____

_____

13. Give students time to use the atlas and make all of their matches.
14. Call on pairs of students to share a match from the "Matching Coordinates" (RS 2.5.2) with the class. Students should be able to explain how they arrived at their conclusion by sharing how to use the coordinates to find the answer.

Closure:

15. After the pairs have shared their ideas, collect the "Matching Coordinates" (RS 2.5.2) from the students and tell them that they have work to do on their own before the next media class. Explain that students need to interview their family members about their family, and figure out where they are from. Maybe their grandparents came from a small town in Maine, or perhaps their mother moved from Ethiopia, or their father from London. It will be the student's job to gather this information and bring it to the next media class.
16. Distribute the "My Family" (WS 2.5.2) interview sheet. Tell students to be sure and bring back the completed sheet to the next class.

Evidence of Understanding:

Embedded AASL Self-Assessment Strategies: ___.___.___: _____

_____

Check for class participation throughout the lesson. Circulate through the room as students work together to complete the "Matching Coordinates" (RS 2.5.2) activity to make sure they are working with their partner and to help when students ask for assistance.

Enrichment Using Technology:

For more practice, have students go try out the latitude and longitude game at GeoKids! (http://www.kidsgeo.com/geography-games/latitude-longitude-map-game.php).

Extension:

1. Read *The Man Who Made Time Travel* by Kathryn Lasky (New York: Farrar, Straus, and Giroux, 2003) or *Sea Clocks: The Story of Longitude* by Louise Borden (New York: Margaret K. McElderry, 2004). Both books are about a man named John Harrison who solved the problem of determining longitude. Discuss with students how the concept of longitude has changed the way we see the world today.

Suggested Modifications:

For students with special needs, reduce the number of coordinate matches for the "Matching Coordinates" (RS 2.5.2) game. Only give these students three or four matching pairs out of the eight matches.

PEDRO'S POSTCARD

Dear _____,

The weather here has been fantastic! I hear your students are studying atlases and how to use coordinates, my favorite! I've included the coordinates of my location on this postcard to see if they can figure out where I live on the map, but first a few clues . . .

The name of my state in Mexico is the same as a popular brand of hot sauce, and the word means, "place where the soil is humid." I live in a tropical atmosphere all year round. In October of 2007, my capital city, Villahermosa (meaning "beautiful village"), suffered from a very large flood, which caused hundreds of thousands of people to move to different areas of the state. The Gulf of Mexico borders my state to the north, and the South American country Guatemala is my bordering neighbor to the east.

Have a great school year!

Sincerely,

Pedro

Coordinates 17° N, 92° W

From *Destination Collaboration 2: A Complete Reference Focused Curriculum Guidebook to Educate 21st Century Learners in Grades 3–5* by Danielle N. DuPuis and Lori M. Carter. Santa Barbara, CA: Libraries Unlimited. Copyright © 2011.

POSTCARD TEMPLATE

Coordinates _____ , _____

Name: _____

Country: _____

Name: _____

Self-Assessment Questions	Yes	Partly	No
My work is neat.			
I have included at least five clues in my postcard			
The "My Family" sheet was helpful when completing this activity.			
The atlas was helpful when completing this activity.			
I have written my name and location on the side and back of the postcard.			

Which map(s) were the most helpful? Why? _____

_____

_____

MATCHING COORDINATES

Hong Kong, China	Dublin, Ireland
Cairo, Egypt	Bombay, India
Auckland, New Zealand	Kingston, Jamaica
Nagasaki, Japan	Baltimore, Maryland U.S.A.

53°N, 6°W	22°N, 114°E
30°N, 31°E	19°N, 72°E
36°S, 174°E	17°N, 76°W
32°N, 129°E	39°N, 76°W

MATCHING COORDINATES ANSWER KEY

Place Name	Matching Coordinates
Dublin, Ireland	53° N, 6° W
Hong Kong, China	22° N, 114° E
Cairo, Egypt	30° N, 31° E
Bombay, India	19° N, 72° E
Auckland, New Zealand	36° S, 174° E
Kingston, Jamaica	17° N, 76° W
Nagasaki, Japan	32° N, 129° E
Baltimore, Maryland, U.S.A.	39° N, 76° W

MY FAMILY

Dear Family,

In my media lessons, I am learning how to use coordinates in order to locate places in an atlas. Next week, I'll be locating the place of our family's origin on the map. I was hoping to have just a few minutes of your time to learn a little about our family's history.

1. Where was I born? _____

2. Where were my parents born? _____

3. Where were my grandparents born? _____

4. Is there a specific event that brought us to the place we live in now? _____
   _____

5. Are there any important things you remember or remember hearing about our family's
   place of origin? _____
   _____

- -

Dear Family,

In my media lessons, I am learning how to use coordinates in order to locate places in an atlas. Next week, I'll be locating the place of our family's origin on the map. I was hoping to have just a few minutes of your time to learn a little about our family's history.

1. Where was I born? _____

2. Where were my parents born? _____

3. Where were my grandparents born? _____

4. Is there a specific event that brought us to the place we live in now? _____
   _____

5. Are there any important things you remember or remember hearing about our family's
   place of origin? _____
   _____

5TH-GRADE LESSONS

LESSON 2: LOCATION NATION

Coordinate! Students will create their own postcards containing hints and coordinates of a place from which their family originated. A tear-off portion of the postcard allows every student to mark his or her spot on a world map. Great discussions can ensue as students look at the world map and see where each of their families originated. *Coordinate* by sharing the tear-off portions of the worksheet with the classroom teacher. Students can mark a map in their classroom showing the various places from around the world where their families originated.

Cooperate! After students have created their own postcards, which contain hints and coordinates of a place their family originated, *cooperate* by offering to share the completed "Postcard Template" (WS 2.5.1) with the classroom teacher. The classroom teacher may wish to use them in a center activity in which students can select a card to practice their atlas skills.

Lesson Plan

Integrated Goals:

Standard 12. Students use spoken, written, and visual language to accomplish their own purposes (e.g., for learning, enjoyment, persuasion, and the exchange of information).

Social Studies

III People, Places, & Environments

c. use appropriate resources, data sources, and geographic tools such as atlases, databases, grid systems, charts, graphs, and maps to generate, manipulate, and interpret information.

Library Media

AASL 21st Century Standards

> **Standard 3:** Share knowledge and participate ethically and productively as members of our democratic society.

Essential Questions:

> How can atlases provide the end user with a variety of information about different places around the world?
>
> How do coordinates assist you when looking for a place on a map?

CLASSROOM CONNECTIONS

Using the "Postcard Template" (WS 2.5.1) students create, classroom teachers could make a class graph or chart to display how many families come from different continents or countries in their class.

Desired Understandings:

Students will understand:

How to use different types of maps to locate information in an atlas.
How to determine when to use different types of maps in an atlas.
How to use coordinates to locate places in an atlas.

Integrated Objectives:

- Students will create a postcard about their family's place of origin, providing coordinates so that classmates can pinpoint their location.

Time Required:

45 minutes

Provided Materials:

- "Postcard Template" (WS 2.5.1)—one per student
- "My Family" (WS 2.5.2)—Students should bring these from the previous class.
- "My Family Sample" (RS 2.5.4)
- "Postcard Template Sample" (RS 2.5.3) (color version available online)

Materials You Will Need to Obtain:

- Computer
- Projection device
- Pencils
- Class set of atlases
- Wall-sized world map

Lesson Procedures:

Engagement:

1. Bring in an artifact from your own family history to share with the class. Some examples are photographs, clothing, musical instruments, souvenirs, and so forth. Give students hints about where your family is from. Using a wall map, have students guess from which country your family originated.

Activity:

2. Distribute an atlas to each student. After sharing with the class where your family originated, tell students to use the atlases to locate the coordinates for your family's city or country of origin. Test the students' answers.

Embedded AASL Skills Indicator: ___.___.___: _____

_____

3. Tell students that they will be writing a postcard to their classroom teacher. Students will use the answers they received from their family interview and will use the "My Family" (WS 2.5.2) interview sheet to assist them in the assignment. In their postcard, students should include clues and information about where their

family originated, and they should also provide the coordinates. However, the students should not give away the answer in their clues. The postcard will serve as part of a class guessing game.

Transition:

4. Distribute copies of the "Postcard Template" (WS 2.5.1).
5. Display "My Family Sample" (RS 2.5.4) and "Postcard Template Sample" (RS 2.5.3). Show students how the information from the "My Family Sample" (RS 2.5.4) interview sheet was used to create the "Postcard Template Sample" (RS 2.5.3).

Activity:

6. Be sure and point out all of the required details of the postcard. Explain that students will be creating clues based on their "My Family" (WS 2.5.2) interview sheet. Students should try and create at least five clues. Also be sure and tell students to write the name of the country or state their clues are about on the back of the postcard, as well as on the side of the postcard in the space provided.

Embedded AASL Responsibilities Indicator: ___.___.___: _____

_____

Embedded AASL Dispositions in Action Indicator: ___.___.___: _____

_____

7. Give students time to complete the activity.
8. Students should trim off the portion to the right of the postcard to use for the sharing session at the end of the class.
9. Explain to students that the postcards will be used to practice using coordinates in either their classrooms or the media center.

Closure:

Embedded AASL Self-Assessment Strategies: ___.___.___: _____

_____

10. When students have completed their postcard, they should assess how they did by completing the bottom portion of the "Postcard Template" (WS 2.5.1).
11. Invite students to come up to the front of the class one at a time to share a clue from their postcard as they place their origin marker on a world or state map.

Evidence of Understanding:

Grade the top and bottom portions of the "Postcard Template" (WS 2.5.1) worksheets and check that students have successfully been able to apply the atlas to locate their own family's origin on a map.

Technology Integration:

Technology

NETS-S

3. Research and Information Fluency

Students apply digital tools to gather, evaluate, and use information. Students:

b. locate, organize, analyze, evaluate, synthesize, and ethically use information from a variety of sources and media.

   Have students create their own hint and make an electronic postcard using ReadWrite-Think's postcard maker (http://www.readwritethink.org/materials/postcard/).

Extension:

Allow students time to explore maps and cool facts around the world in the National Geographic Xpeditions Hall (http://www.nationalgeographic.com/xpeditions/hall/).

Suggested Modifications:

For students in need of modification, reduce the number of required clues for the "Postcard Template" (WS 2.5.1).

MY FAMILY SAMPLE

Dear Family,

In my media lessons, I am learning how to use coordinates in order to locate places in an atlas. Next week, I'll be locating the place of our family's origin on the map. I was hoping to have just a few minutes of your time to learn a little about our family's history.

1. Where was I born? ***Baltimore, MD***

2. Where were my parents born? ***Mother: Baltimore, MD; Father, Munich, Germany***

3. Where were my grandparents born? ***Mother's side: Italy; Father's side: Germany***

4. Is there a specific event that brought us to the place we live in now? ***Your father's mother married someone in the military, and they moved to the USA.***

5. Are there any important things you remember or remember hearing about our family's place of origin? ***Your grandmother was alive during the Holocaust and remembers her friends disappearing from school to go into hiding.***

POSTCARD TEMPLATE SAMPLE

Name: Johnny

Country Name: Munich, Germany

Classroom Teacher's Name

Classroom 5 B

Overlook Elementary School

555 Maple Lawn Lane

Glenmont, FL   USA

Coordinates 48° N, 11° E

Dear Classroom Teacher,

My father was born in this country. This country borders two bodies of water to the north, but neither is an ocean. The Rhine River runs through the west of the country. It is Denmark's only bordering neighbor. The Euro is the currency used. My grandmother lived here during the Holocaust. Can you guess my family's country of origin?

Sincerely,

Johnny

Working in Collaboration

Collaboration

Collaborate! True collaboration requires both the library media specialist and the classroom teacher to share in the design of integrated instruction. Collaboration provides you with an excellent opportunity to design inquiry-based learning activities. Here are some ideas for collaborating with the classroom teachers.

5th Grade: Social Studies

Essential Question: How does the diverse culture of our school help to shape our community?

- Have students create and conduct a survey to examine the variety of cultures in their school. Have students select a country to research that is represented in their school. Students can use an atlas to include factual information about the country of their choice. Students can share their information in a schoolwide virtual or face-to-face celebration.

For further information, please visit
www.destinationcollaboration.com

Bibliography

Works Cited

"Abraham Ortelius." Photograph. *Wikimedia Commons.* 22 May 2006. Web. 4 Oct. 2008. <http://commons.wikimedia.org/wiki/Image:Abraham_Ortelius.jpg>.

"Blank map of the United States." Map. *Wikimedia Commons.* 2 Dec. 2007. Web. 4 Oct. 2008. <http://commons.wikimedia.org/wiki/Image:Blank_map_of_the_United_States. PNG>.

"BlankMap-World-alt." Map. *Wikipedia.* 22 Feb. 2007. Web. 22 July 2008. <http://en. wikipedia.org//:BlankMap-World-alt.svg>.

"CIA Political World Map 2002. "Map. *American Memory.* Jan. 2002. Web. 22 July 2008. <http://memory.loc.gov/cgi-bin/query/h?ammem/gmd:@field(NUMBER+@band (g3200+ct002066))>.

"Claudius Ptolemaeus." *Wikimedia Commons.* 6 Nov. 2007. Web. 4 Oct. 2008. <http://com mons.wikimedia.org/wiki/Image:Claudius_Ptolemaeus.jpg>.

"Coasts and Boundaries." Map. *National Atlas of the United States.* 29 Apr. 2008. Web. 22 July 2008. <http://www.nationalatlas.gov/printable/reference.html>.

"Gerardus Mercator." *Wikimedia Commons.* 24 Mar. 2005. Web. 4 Oct. 2008. <http://com mons.wikimedia.org/wiki/Image:Gerardus_Mercator.jpg>.

"Maryland." Map. *National Atlas of the United States.* 29 Apr. 2008. Web. 22 July 2008. <http://www.nationalatlas.gov/asp/popups.asp?imgFile=../printable/images/preview/ reference/pagegen_md.gif&imgw=588&imgh=450>.

"Oil and Natural Gas Production in the United States." Map. *United States Geological Survey.* 9 Sept. 2008. Web. 9 Sept. 2008. <certmapper.cr.usgs.gov/data/noga95/natl/graphic/ uscells1m.pdf>.

"Ortelius World Map 1570." Map. *Wikimedia Commons.* 5 May 2007. Web. 4 Oct. 2008. <http://commons.wikimedia.org/wiki/Image:OrteliusWorldMap.jpeg>.

"Philippine Climate Map." Map. *Wikipedia.* 27 Feb. 2007. Web. 9 Sept. 2008. <http:// en.wikipedia.org/wiki/index.html?curid=9667380>.

"Physical Map of the World." Map. CIA. Apr. 2008. *World Factbook. World Factbook.* 21 Feb. 2008. Web. 9 Sept. 2008. <https://www.cia.gov/library/publications/the-world-fact book/reference_maps/physical_world.html>.

"Political Map of the World." Map. *World Factbook.* 21 Feb. 2008. Web. 9 Sept. 2008. <https:// www.cia.gov///world-factbook/_maps/_world.html>.

"Population Map." Map. *National Atlas of the United States.* 29 Apr. 2008. Web. 9 Sept. 2008. <http://www.nationalatlas.gov/articles/people/IMAGES/65pop_fig3.gif>.

"Rivers and Lakes." Map. *National Atlas of the United States.* 29 Apr. 2008. Web. 22 July 2008. <http://www.nationalatlas.gov/asp/popups.asp?imgFile=../printable/images/preview/ outline/rivers_lakes.gif&imgw=588&imgh=450>.

Sanchez, Luis Miguel Bugallo. Atlas Santiago Toural. Photograph. 2005. Wikimedia Commons. 29 Dec. 2005. Web. 4 Oct. 2008. <http://commons.wikimedia.org/wiki/ Image:Atlas_Santiago_Toural_GFDL.jpg>.

"States and Capitals." Map. *National Atlas of the United States.* 29 Apr. 2008. Web. 22 July 2008. <http://www.nationalatlas.gov/asp/popups.asp?imgFile=./printable/images/preview/ outline/states_capitals.gif&imgw=588&imgh=450>.

"Total Precipitation Map January 22–28, 2006." Map. *Foreign Agricultural Service.* Web. 9 Sept. 2008. <http://www.fas.usda.gov/pecad/weather/US1.GIF>.

Suggested Book Resources

Borden, Louise. *Sea Clocks: The Story of Longitude*. New York: Margaret K. McElderry, 2004. Print.

Lasky, Kathryn. *The Man Who Made Time Travel*. New York: Farrar, Straus, and Giroux, 2003. Print.

Sweeney, Joan. *Me on the Map*. New York: Crown, 1996. Print.

Suggested Web Resources

Burg, Jerome. *Google Lit Trips*. 1 Oct. 2010. Web. 3 Oct. 2010. <http://www.googlelittrips.org>.

"Latitude and Longitude Game." *KidsGeo*. 2008. Web. 27 Dec. 2008. <http://www.kidsgeo.com/geography-games/latitude-longitude-map-game.php>.

"Map Machine." *National Geographic*. National Geographic Society, 2008. Web. 27 Dec. 2008. <http://maps.nationalgrographic.com/map-machine#theme=Street&c=00&sf=187648892.534865>.

"Map Maker." *National Atlas of the United States*. United States Department if the Interior, 27 Oct. 2008. Web 27 Dec. 2008. <http://www.nationalatlas.gov/natlas/Natlasstart.asp>.

"Postcard Creator." *ReadWriteThink*. NCTE, 2007. Web. 27 Dec. 2008. <http://www.readwritethink.org/materials/postcard/>.

"Vacation and Travel Planner." *The Weather Channel*. The Weather Channel Interactive, Inc., 2008. Web. 27 Dec. 2008. <http://www.weather.com/activities/travel/vacationplanner/?from=secondarynav>.

"Xpedition Hall." *Xpeditions*. National Geographic Society, 2008. Web. 27 Dec. 2008. <http://www.nationalgrographic.com/xpeditions/hall/>.

Chapter 3

Almanacs: Using Reference Tools

Introduction

The almanac is an annual reference publication that includes a wide variety of general information relevant to the year. The information in a kid-friendly almanac is displayed in visually vibrant, attention-grabbing layouts that include tables, charts, lists, and short articles. Students enjoy reading these almanacs because they can access a wide assortment of information from one location. Students will learn that an almanac should be used to compare statistical data or find quick facts that will answer their information question. In this chapter, students will use these facts, combined with their own background knowledge and content objectives, to share information with others in innovative ways. The two-lesson units for 3rd, 4th, and 5th grade will assist students in using both print and online almanacs to locate and share information.

From Year to Year

The almanac is a reference tool that can be rather intimidating to use—even for adults. By introducing students to the kid-friendly versions of the almanac, and familiarizing them with the types of facts and information they can find using an almanac, students will be more likely to locate information efficiently and effectively. The lessons in this chapter will expand from year to year to educate students not only on the content of almanacs but also on how to locate information and how to then apply the information learned. The 3rd-grade lessons in this chapter begin with a basic introduction of what can be found in a kid-friendly almanac. Students explore facts and then advertise what they find to other students, thereby promoting almanac use within the school. In the 4th-grade lessons students use both print and online almanacs to locate facts that will jumpstart further research for students to creatively design a magazine to share with the class. The lessons for 5th grade focus on the current year. Students are posed with a problem of gathering relevant facts about the current year to be included in a class time capsule that will be found by future citizens. Students will infer what things and technologies will change in the future. By exposing students to the use of almanacs throughout elementary school, they will be more likely to use almanacs to seek quick, yearly, rapidly-changing information.

Lifelong Library Use

A short time ago, library associates in the public library field were told that 9 times out of 10, the basic customer reference question could be answered by using one of four resources: the encyclopedia, the dictionary, the phone book, and the almanac. A library associate's ability to access the information found in these resources in a short amount of time would greatly improve customer satisfaction. The inquiries haven't changed that dramatically, but the way in which the answers to the inquiries are accessed has placed a new twist on accessing information. A basic search engine can be used to locate just about any sort of information. However, the accuracy, reliability, and speediness of locating information can be greatly compromised if done by an amateur user. A number of failed search attempts using a search engine may discourage students from pursuing future inquiries; however, by providing students with the necessary tools to quickly locate the information they seek—such as teaching them how to use print and online almanacs—students will be more likely to succeed in locating the answers they seek and more likely to pursue future inquiries.

Self-Assessment Strategies

As students look through an almanac, they can assess their own learning. Students are asked to think about their own interests, what topics will be of interest to future investigations, and their own background knowledge. Because almanacs are easily accessible to students and do provide many fast facts that appeal to student interests, several self-assessment strategies develop naturally throughout this chapter. These periodic self-assessment strategies in each lesson give students an opportunity to reflect and reevaluate.

Relevancy

With an increased focus on Web resources, traditional print resources are being glanced over in pursuit of electronic information. However, depending on the experience of the individual, it may be more difficult or cumbersome to locate the desired information to satisfy an information need by only using the Web. The ability to navigate, understand, and apply the use of both print and online almanacs will assist students throughout their lives in their quest for quick and accurate facts. Whether it be to confirm a statistic for a report or to answer the current Jeopardy question, the ability to use almanacs is a great skill to have when pursuing information.

Working in Isolation

Using the almanac is a skill that students will enjoy learning in order to find general annual information quickly. Students should learn how a print almanac is structured and how to use text features before moving on to an online almanac. Online almanacs offer information that is hyperlinked and includes information in a variety of formats—including games. Hyperlinked information gives students another dimension to consider when thinking about how to find information. Be sure that students understand how to use the print almanac and then expand their knowledge to include the dynamics of online almanacs.

Take notice when students have a special interest in a particular topic, and find out what topics they will explore in their class curriculum. Almanacs have the power to excite students on a wide range of subject areas. In fact, almanacs are now being designed to support the content needs of students. For example, *The World Almanac for Kids: Puzzler Decks* is designed to assist students in a specific grade level with either math, world history, U.S. history and geography, the 50 states, reading, phonics, or vocabulary and word play—all content skills. In addition, some almanacs are written to cover specific topics such as hurricanes or animals and pets.

Classroom teachers are required as part of the curriculum to teach their students text feature skills. Kid-friendly almanacs lend themselves to this curriculum need beautifully. By knowing this and thinking about how to use almanacs to help students attain these skills, you are opening the door for future opportunities to coordinate, cooperate, and collaborate. In addition, classroom teachers are responsible for teaching their students how to present information. By using the lessons in this chapter, you will be modeling a variety of ways for students to present information. Share your final products with the classroom teacher. This small gesture could be the cornerstone for initiating future projects or products.

3RD-GRADE LESSONS

LESSON 1: KICK BACK WITH AN ALMANAC

Coordinate! This almanac lesson will introduce students to the use of text features and product advertising. Many of the student-targeted almanacs are colorful, eye-catching, engaging, and filled with kid-friendly facts. *Coordinate* by sharing the suggested Web sites in the materials section of this lesson with the classroom teacher, or suggesting they check out some of the available almanacs in the media center to reinforce teaching text features in the classroom.

Cooperate! Prior to teaching this lesson to students, *cooperate* with the classroom teacher by discussing what students are currently learning. Emphasize the topic currently being studied in the classroom when delivering this lesson. Students will make stronger connections to the content when they are able to learn more about the topic in an almanac.

Lesson Plan

Integrated Goals:

Language Arts

Standard 8. Students use a variety of technological and information resources (e.g., libraries, databases, computer networks, video) to gather and synthesize information and to create and communicate knowledge.

Library Media

AASL 21st Century Standards

Standard 1: Inquire, think critically, and gain knowledge.

Essential Questions:

How can almanacs help you answer basic information questions?
How can text features help you find information in an almanac?

Desired Understandings:

Students will understand:

How to locate information in an almanac to answer general information questions.
How to use text features when searching for information in an almanac.

Integrated Objectives:

• Students will learn how to use an almanac and will understand its purpose.

Time Required:

45 minutes

Provided Materials:
- "You're Getting Warmer" (ORS 3.3.1)
- "Knack for the Almanac" (OER 3.3.1) PowerPoint
- "Kick Back with an Almanac" (WS 3.3.1)—one half sheet per student

Materials You Will Need to Obtain:
- A set of almanacs for kids
- Projection device
- Pencils
- Computer

Prior to the Lesson:

Assemble the "You're Getting Warmer" (ORS 3.3.1) indicator and place in a prominent area at the front of the room. Also, select some slogans popular in the media for sports clothing, drinks, food, restaurants, and so forth, and write them down on a piece of paper, or type them into a document that can be easily displayed during the lesson. If possible, gather photos or the objects themselves to show students after they guess which product goes with which the slogan.

Lesson Procedures:

Engagement:

1. Display the word "almanac."
2. Show students the "You're Getting Warmer" (ORS 3.3.1) indicator. Explain that as students share their ideas about almanacs you will point the arrow to indicate whether their answer was accurate.
3. Ask students to explain what they know about an almanac. Use the "You're Getting Warmer" (ORS 3.3.1) indicator to show whether their answers are accurate.

Activity:

4. Tell students that they will view a PowerPoint about almanacs. Students should evaluate whether their ideas were accurate.
5. Show students the "Knack for the Almanac" (OER 3.3.1) PowerPoint. This PowerPoint is on a timer. Go to the "View Slideshow" option to allow the PowerPoint to play on its own. Depending on the reading level of your students, you may wish to read the slides aloud.
6. Have students share whether their ideas were accurate and what they have learned.
7. Pass out a print kids almanac to each student. If you do not have enough print almanacs, allow students to share.
8. Ask students to look through the almanacs and cite examples for how the information is displayed. Write and display the student's ideas. Encourage students to note that the information is displayed in a colorful and memorable way.

Transition:

9. Ask students if they have heard of the word "slogan" before. Tell students that a slogan is a catchy phrase used to advertise or promote a product or company.
10. Display one of the slogans you selected.

11. Explain to students that a slogan will be displayed, and it will be the student's job to see if they know the product or company that is being advertised.

DISCUSSION OPPORTUNITY

Ask students to share a favorite topic that they would like to see in almanac form. Have students think about what type of information about that topic would be included in the almanac.

Activity:

12. Allow students time to view the slogan on display. Give students an opportunity to guess the product that goes with the slogan. Discuss how advertisements are colorful, factual, and memorable. Have students identify why slogans are a catchy way to grab a consumer's attention. Ask students why an advertisement should have the qualities that make slogans effective.

13. Have students identify the similarities between advertisements for a product and the way information is displayed inside the almanac. Note that *both* display factual information in a colorful and memorable way.

14. Ask students to explain what tools they would use to locate information in the almanac. Use the "You're Getting Warmer" (ORS 3.3.1) indicator again to guide student's answers (index and table of contents). Next, ask students how the information is organized and displayed in the almanac (tables, charts, or graphs). Tell students that they will find a lot of vibrantly displayed facts in world almanacs for kids.

Transition:

15. Ask students to volunteer information they learned about almanacs.
16. Distribute copies of "Kick Back with an Almanac" (WS 3.3.1).

Activity:

Embedded AASL Skills Indicator: ___.___.___: _____

_____

Embedded AASL Dispositions in Action Indicator: ___.___.___: _____

_____

17. Instruct students to record a topic they would like to learn more about on the top of their "Kick Back with an Almanac" (WS 3.3.1) worksheet.
18. Students should then use the almanac to locate three interesting facts about their topic and record these facts on their "Kick Back with an Almanac" (WS 3.3.1) worksheet. Be sure and remind students to record the page number and to cite their source at the bottom of their paper.

Embedded AASL Responsibilities Indicator: ___.___.___: _____

_____

Embedded AASL Self-Assessment Strategies: ___.___.___: _____

_____

19. Explain to students that they will be using the facts they found to display in a poster during the next class. The poster will be designed like an advertisement. It will have a picture and a slogan, and it should share information about their topic in an eye-catching presentation.
20. Show students where to find other almanacs that can be checked out. You may wish to pull these books ahead of time so they are easily accessible to students.

Evidence of Understanding:

Throughout the lesson check that students are successful using the almanac. Collect "Kick Back with an Almanac" (WS 3.3.1) and check that three facts and a citation have been correctly recorded.

Enrichment Using Technology:

Allow students time to explore an online almanac such as Fact Monster's almanac section (http://www.factmonster.com).

Extension:

Allow students to go to the PBS Kids "Don't Buy It, Get Media Smart!" Web site (http://pbskids.org/dontbuyit/advertisingtricks/). Give students time to learn more about how advertisements entice the consumer to purchase their product.

Suggested Modifications:

Students in need of modifications can have the option of writing one interesting fact instead of three.

KICK BACK WITH AN ALMANAC!

Think of a topic you'd like to know more about.

Record the topic here: _____. Find three facts that support your topic in the almanac. Record your facts below.

1. _____
   _____

   Page number: _____

2. _____
   _____

   Page number: _____

3. _____
   _____

   Page number: _____

   This information taken from

   _____
   _____

- -

KICK BACK WITH AN ALMANAC!

Think of a topic you'd like to know more about.

Record the topic here: _____. Find three facts that support your topic in the almanac. Record your facts below.

1. _____
   _____

   Page number: _____

2. _____
   _____

   Page number: _____

3. _____
   _____

   Page number: _____

   This information taken from

   _____
   _____

3RD-GRADE LESSONS

LESSON 2: DID YOU KNOW?

Coordinate! *Coordinate* with the classroom teacher to have this lesson occur when students are learning about text features. Ask the classroom teacher what text features are being taught so they can be emphasized during this lesson. Coordinate sharing the almanacs with the classroom teacher in a classroom center activity to support the classroom curriculum. This would give students additional practice using almanacs and support their understandings of current content topics. Students could incorporate various text features into their poster based on the classroom teacher's criteria.

Cooperate! Discuss the text features students have learned about in the classroom with the classroom teacher. *Cooperate* by creating a list of text feature criteria for students to include in the creation of their "Did You Know" (WS 3.3.2) poster. Share several copies of the "Did You Know" (WS 3.3.2) poster as a template for the teacher to use to create a poster they can share with their own class.

Lesson Plan

Integrated Goals:

Language Arts

Standard 8. Students use a variety of technological and information resources (e.g., libraries, databases, computer networks, video) to gather and synthesize information and to create and communicate knowledge.

Library Media

AASL 21st Century Standards

Standard 2: Draw conclusions, make informed decisions, apply knowledge to new situations, and create new knowledge.
Standard 4: Pursue personal and aesthetic growth.

Essential Questions:

How can almanacs help to answer basic information questions?
How can text features help to find information in an almanac?

Desired Understandings:

Students will understand:

How to locate information in an almanac to answer general information questions.
How to use text features when searching for information in an almanac.

Integrated Objectives:

- Students will learn how to use an almanac and will understand its purpose.
- Students will use the facts they gathered in the almanac to further pursue their interests.

Time Required:

45 minutes

Provided Materials:

- "Did You Know? Sample" (ORS 3.3.2)
- "Did You Know?" (WS 3.3.2)—one per student
- "Kick Back with an Almanac" (WS 3.3.1)—completed from the previous class

Materials You Will Need to Obtain:

- Computer
- Projection device
- Pencils
- Students should have prior knowledge of how to conduct a search in the public access catalog.
- Access to the public access catalog for student use
- Crayons or colored pencils
- Rulers

Prior to the Lesson:

Gather photos or objects of the products selected to be used in the previous lesson to share with students as part of the engagement activity and place them on display.

Lesson Procedures:

Engagement:

1. Display the products or photos of the products you selected to share with the class. Ask students to recall the slogans for the products.
3. Discuss each company's choices in slogan and packaging of their products with the students. Why do the slogans work? How is the packaging eye-catching? Be sure to explain how each slogan refers to the consumers need for the product. (Example: Nike's slogan "Just Do It" refers to the consumer's need to exercise, and the slogan is meant to suggest that purchasing Nike products will get you to exercise.)

Activity:

4. Remind students that they will use the facts from the almanac that they located in the previous class to create a factual poster. Students should use some of the advertising techniques mentioned during the engagement (catchy slogans, colorful packaging, font choice, etc.) to create a unique and eye-catching poster.
5. Display the "Did You Know? Sample" (ORS 3.3.2) to the class. Point out that the sample includes a catchy title, a related picture, a table, accurate information from the almanac, different colored fonts, a question that inspires the information consumer to think about the poster's information, and a simple citation.

6. Distribute the completed "Kick Back with an Almanac" (WS 3.3.1) worksheets from the previous class.
7. Explain to students while the almanac is a great place to locate fast facts, it also inspires us to learn more about various subjects.
8. Tell students that they should use the public access catalog to locate more information about their topic to support the almanac facts they will use for their poster.

Transition:

9. Distribute the "Did You Know?" (WS 3.3.2) poster templates to each student.
10. Give students access to the public access catalog to locate a book about their topic.

Activity:

11. Give students time to look up and locate a book about their topic in the public access catalog. Students should use the book to gain further understandings about the facts they located in the almanac on their topic.

Embedded AASL Skills Indicator: ___.___.___: _____

_____

Embedded AASL Dispositions in Action Indicator: ___.___.___: _____

_____

12. Encourage students to lightly sketch their ideas on the paper using a pencil. Students may also use rulers to create a table if necessary. Once they are satisfied with their design, students should then add color and complete their poster.
13. Allow students time to create their poster.

Embedded AASL Skills Indicator: ___.___.___: _____

_____

14. Students may choose to create their poster using paper, pencils, color pencils, and/or crayons.
15. Remind students to be sure and cite the almanac they used as well as the book they used to help them in the creation of their poster.

Embedded AASL Responsibilities Indicator: ___.___.___: _____

_____

Closure:

16. After students have completed their poster, have students turn the poster over and complete the self-assessment on the back of their poster.

Embedded AASL Self-Assessment Strategies: ___.___.___: _____

_____

17. Ask students to share their work along with their ideas for using almanacs for future investigations of other topics.

Evidence of Understanding:

Collect the "Did You Know?" (WS 3.3.2) posters and assess for students' ability to gather factual information from the almanac and book resources and to demonstrate how they have gained new understandings with an eye-catching, accurate display. Information should include a catchy title, related picture, a table, accurate information from the almanac, different colored fonts, a question that inspires the information consumer to think about the poster's information, and a simple citation. Use the rubric on the back of the "Did You Know?" (WS 3.3.2) worksheet to grade the posters. Display the completed posters in your school. Other students will enjoy learning random interesting facts from the almanac.

Technology Integration:

Technology

NETS-S

6. Technology Operations and Concepts

Students demonstrate a sound understanding of technology concepts, systems, and operations. Students:

b. select and use applications effectively and productively.

Option 1: Have students share their information by creating a podcast. Visit http://audacity.sourceforge.net or consider having students create a podcast using GarageBand if you own the software.

Option 2: Provide students with computers or laptops with the electronic version of the "Did You Know?" (OEWS 3.3.1) poster. Explain that they may wish to consider using Word-Art for their title and creating a table or text box in order to display their information. Students may also choose to change font colors in order to create an attractive poster.

Extension:

Have students do their own school wide survey about a topic of their choosing. Students can tally and share the results of their survey on the morning announcements or in the school newsletter.

Suggested Modifications:

Print out a copy of the "Did You Know? Sample" (ORS 3.3.2) to give to students in need of further modeling of the project. This will give these students easy access to the example.

DID YOU KNOW?

Name: _____

SELF-ASSESSMENT QUESTIONS

1. Why did you select the facts you chose to share on your "Did You Know?" poster?

   _____

   _____

2. What new understandings did you learn about your topic?

   _____

   _____

3. How was the almanac helpful?

   _____

   _____

4. Would you use an almanac again in the future? For what purpose?

   _____

   _____

Expectations	Not met (1)	Almost there (2)	Great job! (3)
The "Did You Know" poster included accurate information from the almanac.	The information included was inaccurate	Some of the information included was accurate	All of the information included was accurate
The "Did You Know?" poster included visual aides (table, picture, colored fonts).	Many of the visual aides were not included, making the poster difficult to understand	While many of the needed visual aides were included, there is still room for improvement	Image related to the subject, a table, and appropriate fonts are included and add interest to the poster
The "Did You Know" poster included a "catchy title" that encourages others to read the poster.	The title is missing or no attempt was made to create a title that would encourage others to read the poster	An attempt was made to create a "catchy title"	A "catchy title" was created. The title was clever, added interest, and encourages others to read the poster
The "Did You Know?" poster included a source citation.	A source citation was not included	A source citation was included, but was incomplete	An accurate and complete source citation was included

Working in Collaboration

Collaborate! True collaboration requires both the library media specialist and the classroom teacher to share in the design of integrated instruction. Collaboration provides you with an excellent opportunity to design inquiry-based learning activities. Here are some ideas for collaborating with the classroom teachers.

3rd Grade: Social Studies

Essential Question: How can almanacs assist me in gaining an understanding of geography and social studies topics?

- After introducing students to a new social studies topic, give students an opportunity to explore the almanac in regards to geography. Have students explore a country that interests them. Have them look up facts about the country's population, area, religion, and so forth. Students can compare the countries to our own and discuss similarities and differences.

> For further information, please visit
> www.destinationcollaboration.com

4TH-GRADE LESSONS

LESSON 1: MAGAZINE MANIA!

 **Coordinate!** Post the links for the online almanacs listed in the materials section of this lesson on your school media Web site. *Coordinate* with the classroom teacher by sharing where these bookmarks are located so they can be easily accessed and used in the classroom when the teacher needs additional resources for a student project.

 **Cooperate!** After students complete this lesson, *cooperate* with the classroom teacher by sharing the magazine articles students created. Offer to extend the experience by sharing how to look up information in an online magazine database based on topics students have identified as areas of interest they would like an opportunity to investigate.

Lesson Plan

Integrated Goals:

Language Arts

Standard 8. Students use a variety of technological and information resources (e.g., libraries, databases, computer networks, video) to gather and synthesize information and to create and communicate knowledge.

Technology

NETS-S

3. Research and Information Fluency

Students apply digital tools to gather, evaluate, and use information. Students:

b. locate, organize, analyze, evaluate, synthesize, and ethically use information from a variety of sources and media.

Library Media

AASL 21st Century Standards

   Standard 1: Inquire, think critically, and gain knowledge.

Essential Questions:

   How can almanacs help to answer basic information questions?
   How is searching for information in print and online almanacs different?

Desired Understandings:

Students will understand:

How to locate information in both print and online almanacs to answer general information questions.

Integrated Objectives:

- Students will learn how to use an almanac and will understand its purpose.
- Students will use almanacs in multiple formats to locate information.

Time Required:

45 minutes

Provided Materials:

- "Magazine Mania" (OER 3.4.1) PowerPoint
- "Magazine Mania Student Groups" grouping cards (MN 3.4.1)—one per student.
- *Note:* not all cards need to be used; pick and choose which cards you wish to use with your class.
- "Magazine Planner" (WS 3.4.1)—one per student

Materials You Will Need to Obtain:

- Computer
- Projection device
- Pencils
- Computers available for student use
- A set of almanacs for kids
- Access to online versions of
    - Old Farmer's Almanac for Kids (http://www.almanac4kids.com)
    - The World Almanac for Kids (http://worldalmanacforkids.com)
    - Fact Monster—Almanac section (http://www.factmonster.com)
- A variety of children's magazines from the media center

CLASSROOM CONNECTIONS

Share with students that the links to the almanacs are on the school media Web site. Tell students they can access these links from home to assist them in completing their homework.

Lesson Procedures:

Engagement:

1. Display magazines from your media center in the instructional area for students to see as they enter the room. As students enter, act as though you are disappointed with your display. Exclaim: "I just don't seem to have enough magazines for all 4th-grade students!" Pretend as though you just thought of a great idea! Tell students that perhaps they can help by creating their own magazine to add to the collection.

Activity:

2. Tell students that magazines are publications that can contain drawings and photographs, essays, stories, and poems, all by various artists and authors. Different types of magazines can focus on a particular subject or topic such as sports, games, pets, current events, and so forth.

3. Ask students to share some types of magazines of which they are aware. Some examples may include *Nickelodeon Magazine, Ranger Rick, Cricket, Ladybug, Highlights, Sports Illustrated for Kids,* and so forth. Ask students to explain what types of information can be found in a magazine (facts and opinions about various topics).

4. Explain to students that you are interested in having them create some magazines to add to your media center's collection. Explain to students that these magazines will need to be of high interest to students. The magazines should be small so they are more portable for students.

5. Show students the "Magazine Mania" (OER 3.4.1) PowerPoint.

6. Assign students to a team and assign each team a theme for their magazine by distributing the "Magazine Mania Student Groups" (MN 3.4.1) grouping cards.

Transition:

7. Allow students time to find their group.

8. Take some time to review the structure of a few of the magazines with the students. Point out the cover, colorful photographs and pictures, titles, and stories. Discuss why these parts help create an inviting magazine for students. Point out that each article is based on fact but may also contain some of the author's personal opinion.

Activity:

9. Distribute copies of the "Magazine Planner" (WS 3.4.1) to each student in the group.

10. Explain to students that they will be working with the students in their group to create a mini magazine based on one of the theme topics found in an almanac. Each student will be responsible for finding information based on their group's topic and recording it their "Magazine Planner" (WS 3.4.1).

11. Provide students with almanacs and/or online access to almanac Web sites. Remind students to cite the sources they use. Please note: if you opt to use almanac Web sites with your class, you will need to demonstrate how to navigate each Web site.

Embedded AASL Skills Indicator: ___.___.___: _____

_____

Embedded AASL Dispositions in Action Indicator: ___.___.___: _____

_____

Embedded AASL Responsibilities Indicator: ___.___.___: _____

_____

12. Show students how to locate information on their particular theme using the index and table of contents.
13. Give students time to complete the notes portion of the "Magazine Planner" (WS 3.4.1) worksheet.
14. Remind students to work with the other member(s) of their group. Students should use one another as a resource and should collaborate as they complete their "Magazine Planner" (WS 3.4.1).

Embedded AASL Responsibilities Indicator: ___.___.___: _____

---

15. After students complete their notes in the "Magazine Planner" (WS 3.4.1), students should use their notes to write an article on the topic they researched.
16. Give students time to write their articles.

Closure:

17. Collect the "Magazine Planner" (WS 3.4.1) worksheets. Explain that students will use their "Magazine Planner" (WS 3.4.1) to create a mini magazine with their group during the next class.
18. As students are dismissed, ask them to share the kinds of facts they found for their almanac theme. Ask students to share some of their own interests that they would like to find more information about in an almanac.

Embedded AASL Self-Assessment Strategies: ___.___.___: _____

Evidence of Understanding:

Walk around the room as student groups are working to assess their ability to complete the task. Also assess their ability to work in a group successfully.

Technology Integration:

Technology

NETS-S

6. Technology Operations and Concepts

Students demonstrate a sound understanding of technology concepts, systems, and operations. Students:

  a. understand and use technology systems.

In order to complete the mini magazine, students can also use the "Stapleless Book" on http://www.readwritethink.org. Click on "Student Materials" to find the link for the book.

Extension:

1. Create a classroom wiki for your library media center using http://www.wiki spaces.com. Create a space for your 4th-grade students to update interesting facts found in their almanacs. Consider adding this link to the school Web page. This could be an ongoing "Did YOU Know?" area for interested students to explore.

Suggested Modifications:

Students in need of modifications should be paired with students who are independent. Consider using the technology option for students who enjoy using the computer.

MAGAZINE MANIA STUDENT GROUPS

Language	Government
Measurement	Math
Technology	Fashion
Animals	Health
Science	Environment
Weather	Holidays

History	Transportation
Religion	Television
Movies/Birthdays	Space
Nations	Calendars
Sports	Disasters
Geography	Intentionally blank

MAGAZINE PLANNER

Name: _____

Directions: Record your notes on the lines below. Next, using your creativity, your notes, and what you know from your brain, write a well-written article about your assigned theme.

Names of group members: _____

_____

Our magazine theme: _____

Notes: _____

_____

_____

_____

_____

_____

_____

_____

_____

_____

_____

Almanac citations: _____

_____

_____

_____

_____

_____

_____

_____

_____

_____

_____

_____

_____

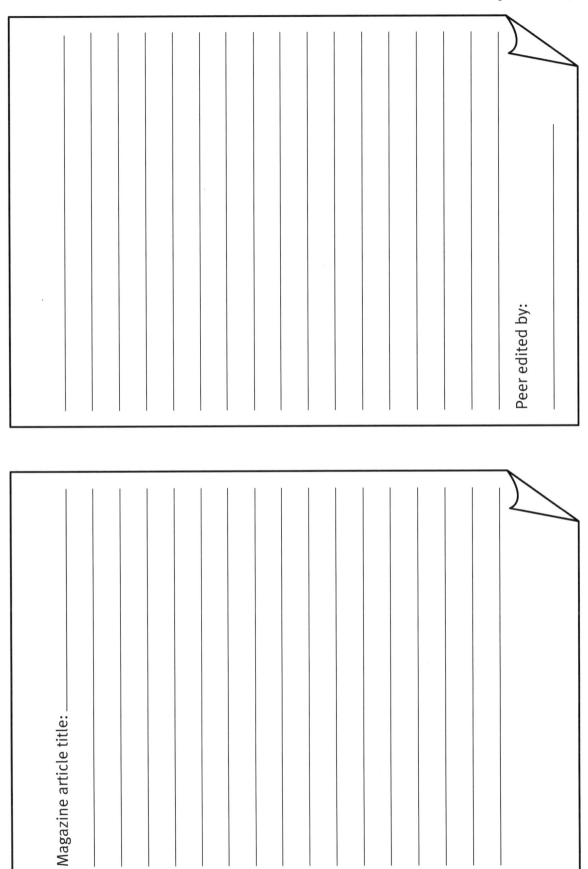

Peer edited by: _____

Magazine article title: _____

4TH-GRADE LESSONS

LESSON 2: START THE PRESSES

Coordinate! In the extension activity, students are encouraged to ethically post information they learned from an almanac on a school wiki. *Coordinate* by sharing the wiki Web address with the classroom teacher so that students can continue to learn from almanacs and each other as they explore other topics in the classroom.

Cooperate! Prior to teaching this lesson, *cooperate* with the classroom teacher by sharing the activities students will complete during this lesson. The classroom teacher may wish to teach students how to properly edit a written work using proofreading symbols for spelling, capitalization, punctuation, and grammar usage. Students will be better prepared to peer-edit their "Magazine Planner" (WS 3.4.1) if they have already had prior editing experience and practice in the classroom.

Lesson Plan

Integrated Goals:

Language Arts

Standard 8. Students use a variety of technological and information resources (e.g., libraries, databases, computer networks, video) to gather and synthesize information and to create and communicate knowledge.

Standard 12. Students use spoken, written, and visual language to accomplish their own purposes (e.g., for learning, enjoyment, persuasion, and the exchange of information).

Library Media

AASL 21st Century Standards

   Standard 2: Draw conclusions, make informed decisions, apply knowledge to new situations, and create new knowledge.

Essential Questions:

   How can almanacs help to answer basic information questions?
   How is searching for information in print and online almanacs different?

Desired Understandings:

Students will understand:

   How to locate information in both print and online almanacs to answer general information questions.

Integrated Objectives:

* Students will learn how to use an almanac and will understand its purpose.
* Students will use almanacs in multiple formats to locate information.

Time Required:

45 minutes

Provided Materials:

- "Mini Magazine" (WS 3.4.2)—one per student group—for accessibility purposes these should not be stapled until after students have completed their work.
- "Magazine Planner" (WS 3.4.1)—one per student completed from the previous lesson

Materials You Will Need to Obtain:

- A set of almanacs for kids
- Access to online versions of
  - Old Farmer's Almanac for Kids (http://www.almanac4kids.com)
  - The World Almanac for Kids (http://worldalmanacforkids.com)
  - Fact Monster—Almanac section (http://www.factmonster.com)
- Colored pencils and crayons
- Pencils

Lesson Procedures:

Engagement:

1. Select a few of the "Magazine Planner" (WS 3.4.1) worksheets completed in the previous class to share. Point out well-written stories that include effective titles and interesting facts.

Activity:

2. Display a copy of the "Mini Magazine" (WS 3.4.2).
3. Explain to students that they are taking the information from their "Magazine Planner" (WS 3.4.1) and placing it into their group's "Mini Magazine" (WS 3.4.2). Point out that each story has a place for a picture/illustration that should complement the text.

Transition:

4. Pass back the "Magazine Planner" (WS 3.4.1) worksheets completed in the previous lesson.

Activity:

5. Have students swap their "Magazine Planner" (WS 3.4.1) with another person in the class for peer editing—checking for grammar, spelling, punctuation, and content.

Embedded AASL Skills Indicator: ___.___.___: _____

> ### DISCUSSION OPPORTUNITY
>
> Use this lesson as an opportunity to discuss respecting the intellectual property rights of others. Since the students spent time creating their own articles for their mini magazine, hold a discussion about how they would feel if someone else came along and copied their work.

6. After their editing is complete, provide each group with a copy of the "Mini Magazine" (WS 3.4.2).
7. Tell students they should review the comments made by the peers. Students will need to determine whether to accept the changes made by their peer review, reject the changes, or modify them in order to meet the needs of the assignment.

Embedded AASL Self-Assessment Strategies: ___.___.___: _____

_____

8. Give students time to input their edited information onto a page of the "Mini Magazine" (WS 3.4.2).

Embedded AASL Dispositions in Action Indicator: ___.___.___: _____

_____

9. Instruct students to work with their group to create and include a title and illustrations for their "Mini Magazine" (WS 3.4.2).

Embedded AASL Responsibilities Indicator: ___.___.___: _____

_____

10. Students can also include other articles that relate to current classroom content in their "Mini Magazine" (WS 3.4.2).

Closure:

Embedded AASL Self-Assessment Strategies: ___.___.___: _____

_____

11. Collect the "Mini Magazine" (WS 3.4.2) from each group. Ask students to share their "Mini Magazine" (WS 3.4.2) with the class. After students share their magazine, they should use the self-assessment rubric to determine the effectiveness of their product.

Evidence of Understanding:
Check for student participation throughout the lesson.
   Assess each groups "Mini Magazine" (WS 3.4.2) for accurate information, catchy titles, text appropriate pictures, and effective group effort.

Enrichment Using Technology:

1. Continue using the site from http://www.readwritethink.org for completion of this activity. Continue allowing students to work on and finish their "Mini Magazine" by using the "Stapleless Book" option on this site.

Extension:

1. Allow students to continue using the library media center classroom wiki that you created for the first lesson on http://www.wikispaces.com. Encourage students to add images, links, and other resources to their wiki entries.

Suggested Modifications:

For students in need of modifications, distribute the third page of the "Mini Magazine" (WS 3.4.2) to them to record their article. This page has more space between lines and will provide students with additional writing space.

Mini Magazine

_____

_____

Names: _____

_____

Grading Rubric

Expectations	Not met (1)	Almost there (2)	Great job (3)
The mini magazine included accurate information from the almanac	The information included was inaccurate	Some of the information included was accurate	All of the information included was accurate
The mini magazine included visual aides (pictures, colored fonts, etc.)	Many of the visual aides were not included, making the magazine difficult to understand	While several visual aides were included, there is still room for improvement	Several visual aides were included and added interest to the magazine
The mini magazine was created with the effort of all group members	The group did not work well together	The group worked together some of the time to complete the mini magazine	The group consistently worked collaboratively to create the mini magazine
The mini magazine is complete and includes correct source citations	The mini magazine has several blank areas and/or does not include the correct source citation	The mini magazine includes several articles to fill in the spaces of the magazine template and includes a source citation	The mini magazine is complete and contains correct source citations

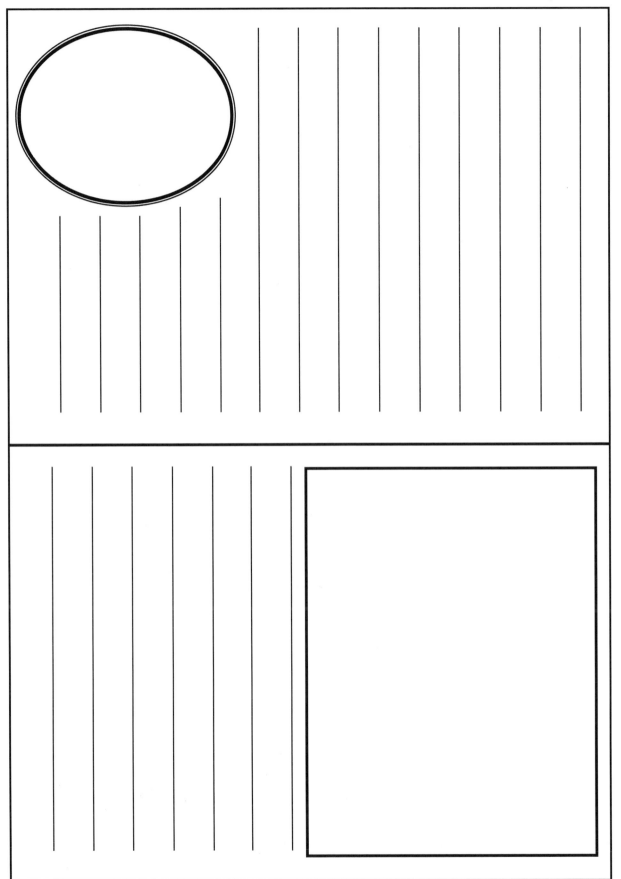

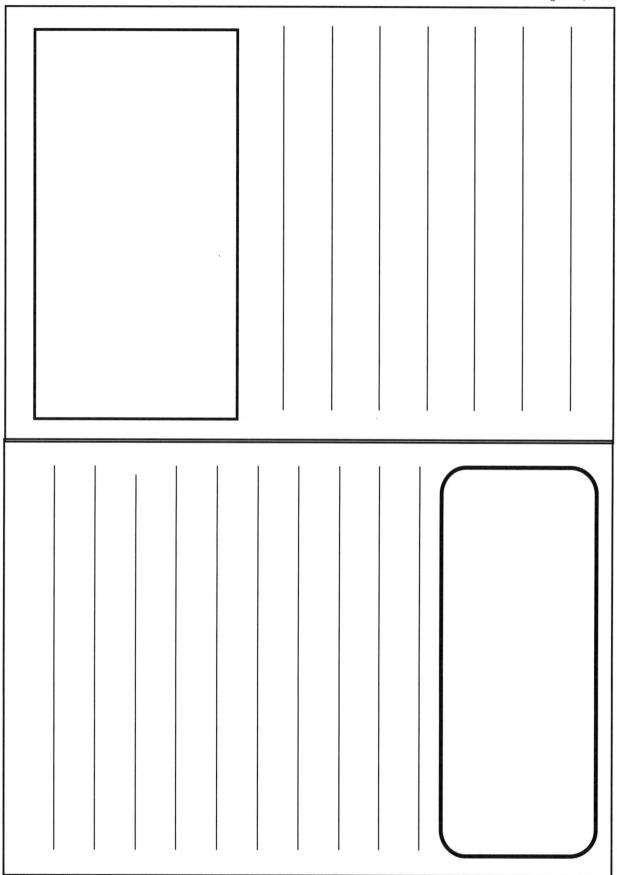

Working in Collaboration

Collaborate! True collaboration requires both the library media specialist and the classroom teacher to share in the design of integrated instruction. Collaboration provides you with an excellent opportunity to design inquiry-based learning activities. Here are some ideas for collaborating with the classroom teachers.

4th Grade: Social Studies

Essential Question: How can almanacs help you understand the quality of life in other countries?

- Have students explore some of the world statistical data in an almanac. Students can work in groups to discuss the data for a country on each continent. Using the data as a guide, students can determine which country might have the highest quality of life and create a presentation about how they came to their conclusion.

For further information, please visit
www.destinationcollaboration.com

5TH-GRADE LESSONS

LESSON 1: TIME STANDS STILL

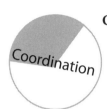

Coordinate! *Coordinate* by finding out what students are studying in the classroom and offer the almanacs for students to use as they begin to explore a research topic. Once students have selected a topic to research from the almanac, provide access to other books and reference materials to assist them as they gather information to complete their project.

Cooperate! Think about ways almanacs can be introduced into the classroom curriculum. *Cooperate* by discussing your ideas with the classroom teacher and sharing some suggestions for online and print almanacs to use with their students. The classroom teacher may also wish to *cooperate* by reading the book suggested in the extension part of this lesson.

Lesson Plan

Integrated Goals:

Language Arts

Standard 12. Students use spoken, written, and visual language to accomplish their own purposes (e.g., for learning, enjoyment, persuasion, and the exchange of information).

Library Media

AASL 21st Century Standards

> **Standard 2:** Draw conclusions, make informed decisions, apply knowledge to new situations, and create new knowledge.
> **Standard 4:** Pursue personal and aesthetic growth

Essential Questions:

> How can almanacs inspire us to learn more?
> How can almanacs answers basic information questions?

Desired Understandings:

Students will understand:

> How to locate information in an almanac.
> When to use an almanac when seeking information.

Integrated Objectives:

- Students will practice using almanacs to locate factual information.

Time Required:

45 minutes

Provided Materials:

- "Facts or Fads?" (WS 3.5.1)—one half sheet per student

Materials You Will Need to Obtain:

- Computer
- Projection device
- Pencils
- Computers for student use
- Access to online versions of (or other similar almanac Web sites)
  - Old Farmer's Almanac for Kids (http://www.almanac4kids.com)
  - The World Almanac for Kids (http://worldalmanacforkids.com)
  - Fact Monster—Almanac section (http://www.factmonster.com)
- Set of almanacs
- Digital camera

Lesson Procedures:

Engagement:

1. Bring in items from your own past when you were of elementary school age to share with the class. These items can include but are not limited to yearbooks, photographs, clothing, jewelry, popular music, technology of the times, and so forth. Share a bit of your own history with the class. Comment on how things have changed from then to now.

Activity:

2. Ask students what they think of these items and allow time to share. Next, pose the question, "I wonder what elementary students 30 years from now would think of the items we have today?"
3. Ask students how we keep record of events and major occurrences that happen year to year. Display copies of almanacs that you have available in your media center. Explain that an almanac is a great resource for annual and recurring facts and events.
4. Tell students that they are going to have an opportunity to collect and document artifacts for a time capsule.
5. Share with students the purpose of a time capsule.

Embedded AASL Skills Indicator: ___.___.___: _____

_____

6. Distribute almanacs to the class for perusal. As they browse, ask students to look for facts that would have the most interest to students 30 years from now.
7. Explain that the facts they find will be included as part of their time capsule.

Transition:

8. Distribute the "Facts or Fads?" (WS 3.5.1) worksheet to each student. Define the word "fad" for students.

Embedded AASL Dispositions in Action Indicator: ___.___.___: _____

_____

9. Allow students time to look through the print and online almanacs to find three facts or fads to include on their worksheet. Students should also be sure to explain how their fact or fad relates to our world today.
10. Brainstorm with the class any events, school changes, new teachers, or any new characteristic of the school that could be recorded and included in the time capsule. Record student responses, and save responses to revisit in the next lesson.
11. Explain to students that they will include facts about their school in the time capsule along with images or visual aides so that students of the future will be able to compare and contrast similarities and differences between the past and present.

Closure:

Embedded AASL Responsibilities Indicator: ___.___.___: _____

_____

Embedded AASL Skills Indicator: ___.___.___: _____

_____

Embedded AASL Self-Assessment Strategies: ___.___.___: _____

_____

12. Ask for students to share one of the facts or fads they gathered and how it relates to our world today.
13. Gather students together for a class photo that can be printed for inclusion in the time capsule.

Evidence of Understanding:

Collect the "Facts or Fads?" (WS 3.5.1) worksheet. Check that students included both a fact or fad and an explanation of the chosen fact or fad.

Enrichment Using Technology:

Have students explore the dMarie Time Capsule Web site http://dmarie.com/timecap/. Students can put in any day in history to see what the popular movie titles and songs were as well as the cost of gas per gallon, and so forth.

Extension:

1. Read *We Were Here: A Short History of Time Capsules* by Patricia Seibert (Brookfield, CT: Millbrook Press, 2002). This story will give readers a background history of

time capsules, and how they have made an impact. Instructions on how students can make their own time capsules are included.

Suggested Modifications:

Have students with difficulties create only one cube from the "Facts or Fads?" (WS 3.5.1) worksheet instead of three.

FACTS OR FADS?

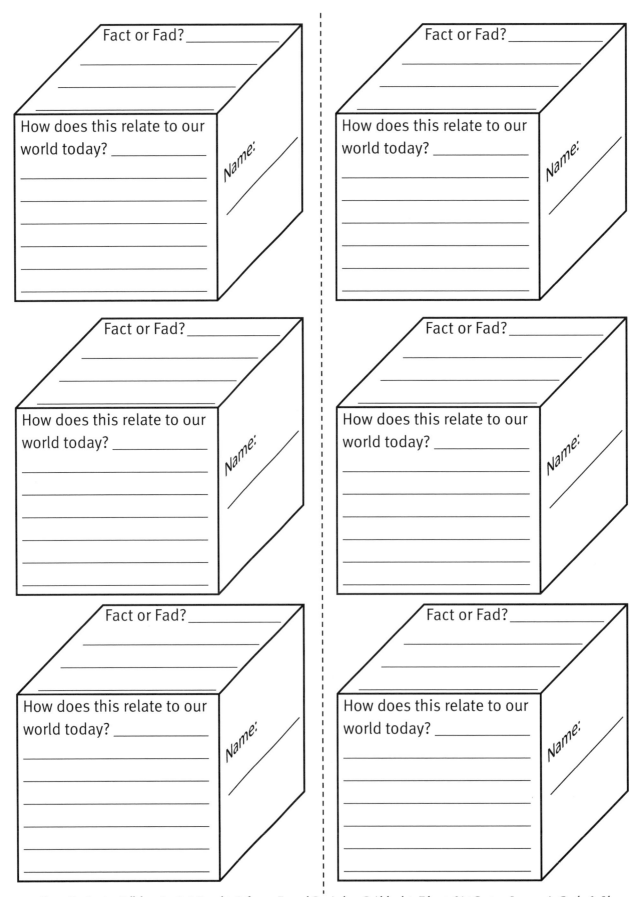

Fact or Fad? _____

_____

_____

How does this relate to our world today? _____

_____

_____

_____

_____

_____

Name: _____

Fact or Fad? _____

_____

_____

How does this relate to our world today? _____

_____

_____

_____

_____

_____

Name: _____

Fact or Fad? _____

_____

_____

How does this relate to our world today? _____

_____

_____

_____

_____

_____

Name: _____

Fact or Fad? _____

_____

_____

How does this relate to our world today? _____

_____

_____

_____

_____

_____

Name: _____

Fact or Fad? _____

_____

_____

How does this relate to our world today? _____

_____

_____

_____

_____

_____

Name: _____

Fact or Fad? _____

_____

_____

How does this relate to our world today? _____

_____

_____

_____

_____

_____

Name: _____

5TH-GRADE LESSONS

LESSON 2: OFF TO THE FUTURE

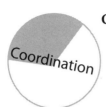

Coordinate! *Coordinate* by sharing this unit with the classroom teacher and sharing the available online almanac links on the school library media Web site. Offer to coordinate the timing of this lesson with classroom instruction on either the use of almanacs or a lesson that covers moments in history.

Cooperate! Gather the materials for creating the time capsule used in this lesson. *Cooperate* by sharing the time capsule project idea with the art teacher. The art teacher may have some suggestions for how the time capsule should be designed. Students can design and create the class time capsule during an art class prior to coming to media.

Lesson Plan

Integrated Goals:

Language Arts

Standard 12. Students use spoken, written, and visual language to accomplish their own purposes (e.g., for learning, enjoyment, persuasion, and the exchange of information).

Library Media

AASL 21st Century Standards

   Standard 3: Share knowledge and participate ethically and productively as members of our democratic society.

Essential Questions:

   How can almanacs inspire us to learn more?
   How can almanacs answer basic information questions?

Desired Understandings:

Students will understand:

   How to locate information in an almanac.
   When to use an almanac when seeking information.

Integrated Objectives:

- Students will use facts from an almanac to create a class time capsule.

Time Required:

45 minutes

> **BUILD YOUR OWN RESOURCE**
>
> Create a Web site in Google Sites or another easy-to-use tool to link to your school Web site as a "time capsule." Each year this lesson is taught, a new page can be added to the site, showing the facts and fads during the time. Future students can go backward in time to learn about the different facts or fads of your school.

Provided Materials:

- "Facts or Fads?" (WS 3.5.1)—completed from previous lesson
- "Time Tag" (WS 3.5.2)—one per student

Materials You Will Need to Obtain:

- Computer
- Projection device
- Pencils
- Time capsule (this can be a box, plastic bin, empty paint can from a hardware store, or any other container you can find.)
- Set of almanacs
- Scissors

Prior to the Lesson:

Prior to students arrival, decorate the time capsule with the class picture from the previous lesson.

Lesson Procedures:

Engagement:

1. Show students the decorated time capsule. Explain that their items will be sealed inside the capsule to be opened by students in their school sometime in the future.

Activity:

Embedded AASL Self-Assessment Strategies: ___.___.___: _____

_____

2. Display the brainstorming list generated in the previous class. Ask students to brainstorm as a class if there is additional information they would like to add, or if there is information that should be modified or rejected. Students should explain their thinking if they are making suggestions for modification or rejection.
3. Distribute the "Time Tag" (WS 3.5.2) worksheet to each student in the class.
4. Explain that each student needs to choose an item from the brainstorming list to write about on their "Time Tag" (WS 3.5.2).
5. Give students time to record their choice on their "Time Tag" (WS 3.5.2).

Embedded AASL Skills Indicator: ___.___.___: _____

_____

6. Students should then explain their choice for inclusion in the time capsule. Explain to students the importance of showing respect for and responding to the ideas of others in a respectful way.

7. Have students use the colored pencils to illustrate their choice. When completed, students should cut out the time tag and their illustration/explanation box from the "Time Tag" (WS 3.5.2) worksheet.

Transition:

8. Distribute string for students to attach their "Time Tag" (WS 3.5.2) to their illustration/explanation box.

Activity:

Embedded AASL Dispositions in Action Indicator: ___.___.___: _____

_____

Embedded AASL Responsibilities Indicator: ___.___.___: _____

_____

9. Have students share their "Time Tag" (WS 3.5.2) with the class.
10. In a ceremonious manner, place the "Facts or Fads?" (WS 3.5.1) sheets from the previous lesson into the time capsule. Instruct students to come up one at a time to lower their "Time Tag" (WS 3.5.1) into the time capsule.
11. Once all students have included their items, seal the time capsule.

Closure:

12. Place the time capsule in a designated place in your media center where it will remain until such a day that it is opened.

Evidence of Understanding:

When students share their "Time Tag" (WS 3.5.2) with the class, check for completion and understanding of the worksheet.

Enrichment Using Technology:

1. Have students use digital cameras to photograph images from around the school to include with their "Time Tag" (WS 3.5.2) and place in the time capsule.

Extension:

1. Have students create a theme-based time capsule in which they research a topic of interest. Students can include photos, audio recordings, and other artifacts based on their topic.

Suggested Modifications:

Assist students with special needs in selecting an item from the brainstormed class list to write about. Instead of drawing a picture on the "Time Tag" (WS 3.5.2), have students think of an object that represents their topic to be included and attached to their explanation.

TIME TAG

Name: _____

Directions: Use the box on the left to create an illustration about an item in the brainstorming list from your class to go in the time capsule. Next, complete the blank tag below, explaining what the illustration is about.

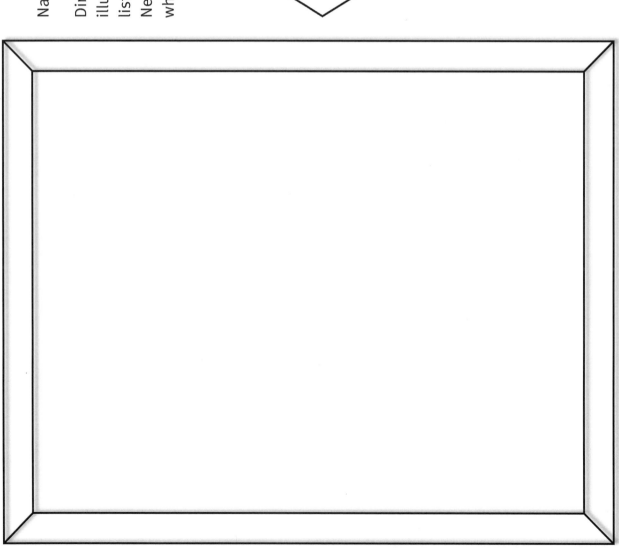

Working in Collaboration

Collaborate! True collaboration requires both the library media specialist and the classroom teacher to share in the design of integrated instruction. Collaboration provides you with an excellent opportunity to design inquiry-based learning activities. Here are some ideas for collaborating with the classroom teachers.

5th Grade: Social Studies

Essential Question: How can almanacs help to preserve our societies past?

- Students could choose a topic of interest to them and research the topic going back in time and reference how and why this topic has changed over time. Students should be guided to choose a narrow topic. Students can create their own timeline showing their topic's progression through history. Infer what might happen regarding their topic in years to come.

For further information, please visit
www.destinationcollaboration.com

Bibliography

Suggested Print Resource

Seibert, Patricia. *We Were Here: A Short History of Time Capsules.* Brookfield: Millbrook, 2002. Print.

Suggested Web Resources

Audacity. 2008. Web. 19 Oct. 2008. <http://audacity.sourceforge.net >.

dMarie Time Capsule. dMarie Direct. 2008. Web. 19 Oct. 2008. <http://dmarie.com/timecap/>.

Don't Buy It: Get Media Smart! KCTS Television. 2004. Web. 19 Oct. 2008. <http://pbskids.org/dontbuyit/advertisingtricks/>.

Fact Monster. Pearson Education. 2007. Web. 19 Oct. 2008. <http://www.factmonster.com/>.

IRA/NCTE. 19 Oct. 2008. Web. 19 Oct. 2008. <http://www.readwritethink.org >.

Old Farmer's Almanac for Kids. 2006. Web. 19 Oct. 2008. <http://www.almanac4kids.com/.php>.

Tangient. 2008. Web. 19 Oct. 2008. <http://www.wikispaces.com. >.

World Almanac for Kids Online. 2008. Web. 19 Oct. 2008. <http://www.worldalmanacforkids.com/>.

Chapter 4

Biographies: Using Reference Tools

Introduction

Biographies hold high interest for students, as they desire to learn more about famous people who have made an important contribution to society. Biographies can hold hidden jewels of inspiration for young people. It is important for students to learn that many people who are heroic or successful may have come from experiences similar or more difficult than their own. Students will learn that many successful people have struggled and persevered on their own life's journey. Reading biographies may encourage students to try new skills. The two-lesson units for 3rd, 4th, and 5th grades will assist students in applying their knowledge of text features, encyclopedias, the public access catalog, and notetaking to give them opportunities to learn more about how they can become contributing, responsible members of our democratic society.

From Year to Year

Biographies are an inspirational book genre. While biographies themselves aren't necessarily considered reference tools, there are many biography references such as databases and encyclopedias that can be used to locate information about various famous people who have made an important contribution to society. Biography book reports are a common assignment in the elementary classroom setting. In fact, students may even choose to write about the same person from one year to the next. The purpose of these lessons is to encourage students to not just learn facts about famous people, but also to understand why the contributions they made to our society are/were so valuable. The lessons in this chapter will build on what was covered in the previous year for students to achieve a true understanding and application into real-world situations. In the 3rd-grade lessons students learn about one another and relate to their classmates through writing a classmate's biography. Fourth-grade lessons incorporate biography books and online resources to learn about a famous American in order to create a fun and educational game about the person they researched. In the 5th-grade lessons, students reflect on the importance of a famous person's life, and then they use what they have learned to create a professional résumé for their famous person. Through their experience in marketing a famous person for a job, students will learn the value of being able to market themselves, as they explore future job opportunities in the real world. Through an examination of the lives of famous people, students can make connections and realize that they too have value and the potential to explore, create, and change our society through their ideas, collaborations, and discoveries.

Lifelong Library Use

There will always be a new discovery, idea, or invention that will change the way we see and experience our ever-growing and -changing society. Our world changes *so* rapidly, it is sometimes difficult to keep up with all of the new changes. People all over the world are making scientific discoveries, creating new educational methods, and inventing technologies that may or may not affect our lives in a positive way. By sharing the importance of biographies with students, they can be more aware of how and why our society transforms as we move forward in our thinking. Modeling the use of online biography resources will assist students as they learn and understand more about the ever-changing world around them. Understanding the people that make up our diverse planet will help students to make more informed decisions, and make them more culturally proficient as they continue to grow into mature and responsible adults. In their quest to become globally aware and responsive, students will utilize library resources, and as a result, they will become a library "believer" and lifelong library user.

Self-Assessment Strategies

Just as the famous people students learn about had to evaluate their own experiments and projects, so must students, so they too can be successful on the career path of their choosing. It is important for students to realize that mistakes can be important life-changing moments. It is through the assessment of our own mistakes that we learn and grow as individuals, just as many of the people in the biography books we read about and discuss. As students explore and read biographies about famous people, it is important to realize there are other sources of information to consult in order to gather all the necessary facts prior to making any conclusions. The self-assessments in this chapter ask students to assess for gaps or weaknesses in their research, adapt their search strategies, recognize new knowledge and understandings, and ask for help as necessary. In using self-questioning and assessing their own learning, students will be better prepared to make changes as they grow into contributing members of society.

Relevancy

Learning about the lives of others and satisfying a natural curiosity for the world around us will always be a relevant topic—to both young students and adults alike. Being educated in ways to not only find information about others, but also to relate and understand why humans do what they do is important as students grow into mature human beings and make decisions independently. Students must attain cultural proficiency skills in order to become collaborative members of a global society. Reading biographies will help students create a tolerance and awareness for various cultures, religions, hardships, and differences in economic status. The understanding of the lives of others gives us insight into our own lives and can even provide us with the inspiration and understanding to change our current path or journey.

Working in Isolation

Biographies and autobiographies have long held high interest for students. Students learn to appreciate the struggle and fortitude often necessary in order to become heroic or successful in life. The magic of reading biographies is learning that famous people have often had to overcome obstacles similar to or more challenging than our own. The power of this realization can be motivating for students. Biographies can intrigue students by showing that a single defining moment can set the course for an individual's life experiences and choices.

Typically, students are lured to biographies of famous people such as celebrities, sports stars, and movie icons. These kinds of biographies may not provide students with a life-changing experience, however, as students select these types of biographies, consider that reading a celebrity's biography may be the window that opens students to the pleasure of reading.

Students must be introduced to other types of biographies, as well. Fill the biography section of the media center with biographies of culturally diverse people, a wide offering of people with historical significance, scientific and mathematical geniuses, young people who have made a difference, and current cultural icons. Choose to read excerpts from biographies in order to share the struggles and defining moments of famous and successful people.

Your students will learn how to conduct an interview in order to create an acceptable biography. Students will read about famous people and use their knowledge to create a game or résumé of a famous person. Share these products with the classroom teacher. This will be a great way to begin a discussion that may lead toward coordination, cooperation, and collaboration.

3RD-GRADE LESSONS

LESSON 1: WHO'S WHO IN OUR CLASS

Coordinate! This lesson introduces students to biographies and autobiographies. Students will interview a classmate to learn more about them in order to create a biography about them. Interviewing is a skill that students will learn as part of reading and language arts. *Coordinate* with the classroom teacher by teaching the skill of interviewing to coincide with the classroom teacher's project idea.

Cooperate! It is common for classroom teachers to assign biography book reports to students. *Cooperate* with the classroom teacher to learn when this project will be assigned. Instead of merely writing a report, students could write an interview dialogue as if they were interviewing the person they read about.

Lesson Plan

Integrated Goals:

Language Arts

Standard 12. Students use spoken, written, and visual language to accomplish their own purposes (e.g., for learning, enjoyment, persuasion, and the exchange of information).

Library Media

AASL 21st Century Standards

Standard 1: Inquire, think critically, and gain knowledge.

Essential Questions:

How can biographies give you greater insights about a famous person who has made an important contribution to society?
How can reading biographies enrich our own lives?

Desired Understandings:

Students will understand:

What information can be found in a biography by participating in their own biographical interview.
How biographies can enrich the lives of those who read them.

Integrated Objectives:

- Students will identify biographies and conduct an interview of a classmate in order to write a short biography about that classmate.

Time Required:

45 minutes

Provided Materials:

- "Interview Tickets" (MN 4.3.1)—one ticket per student. Copy and cut out the tickets. Assign student partners and write the names on the tickets. Be sure to match students together so that both students' names will correspond as the interviewer and interviewee for their tickets.
- "Interview Notebook" (WS 4.3.1)—one per student
- "Student Self-Assessment Strategy" (WS 4.3.3)—one per student

Materials You Will Need to Obtain:

- Computer
- Projection device
- Pencils
- Biography books of a wide variety
- Access to the Web site http://www.biography.com/bio4kids/bio4kids-video.jsp

Prior to the Lesson:

Collect a wide variety of biographies from your school library media center collection. Display the biographies on a table in the front of the library media center. Preview the suggested Web site in the materials and choose a video to share with your students. You may click on "Browse Video List" to choose a particular video from the "Defining Moments" collection.

Lesson Procedures:

Engagement:

1. Display the Web site http://www.biography.com/bio4kids/bio4kids-video.jsp. Allow students time to view the "Defining Moments" online video that you selected.
2. After the video has ended, ask students, "What was the defining moment in this person's life that caused them to become famous?" Allow students to answer and accept all appropriate answers.

Activity:

Embedded AASL Skills Indicator: ___.___.___: _____

3. Explain to students that they will be learning about a kind of book that tells about the life and times of a famous person. Ask students if they know what kind of book tells about a person's life (biography). Briefly explain the difference between a biography and an autobiography. Tell students that they just listened to a short video biography about a famous person. Ask students how they think the author of the video biography got the information about the famous person in order to create the video (conduct an interview, research other resources about that person).

4. Show students how to conduct a simple interview by asking a student in the class a few simple questions and taking notes as the student answers. The notes should be displayed to model proper interviewing and notetaking skills to students in the class.

Embedded AASL Skills Indicator: ___.___.___: _____

_____

5. Ask students to brainstorm some questions to ask their classmates in a biographical interview.
6. Explain to students that they will be conducting an interview to learn more about a classmate.
7. Tell students that they will use this interview in order to write a simple biography about their classmate.
8. Explain that each student will be given a ticket with the name of a classmate. After the tickets are distributed, each student should find their partner.

Transition:

9. Distribute the "Interview Tickets" (MN 4.3.1) and ask students to locate and sit with their partner.

Activity:

10. Distribute the "Student Self-Assessment Strategy" (WS 4.3.3) and "Interview Notebook" (WS 4.3.1) to each student.

Embedded AASL Dispositions in Action Indicator: ___.___.___: _____

_____

11. Read the interview questions to the students. Discuss appropriate responses for each question. After looking at the questions on the first two pages of the "Interview Notebook" (WS 4.3.1), instruct students to answer the first two questions in the "Student Self-Assessment Strategy" (WS 4.3.3).

Embedded AASL Dispositions in Action Indicator: ___.___.___: _____

_____

Embedded AASL Responsibilities Indicator: ___.___.___: _____

_____

12. Give students time to conduct their interviews and record their information into the "Interview Notebook" (WS 4.3.1).

13. Walk around the room to make yourself available should students require assistance.

Closure:

Embedded AASL Self-Assessment Strategies: ___.___.___: _____

_____

14. Ask students to take a look at their interview sheets to makes sure there are no unanswered questions. Give students an opportunity to ask the interviewee a question they might have missed.
15. Ask students to share some of their interview answers with the class.
16. Collect the "Interview Notebook" (WS 4.3.1) from each student.

Evidence of Understanding:

Collect and check to see that students were able to successfully conduct an interview of their classmate and complete their "Interview Notebook" (WS 4.3.1).

Technology Integration:

Technology

NETS-S

3. Research and Information Fluency

Students apply digital tools to gather, evaluate, and use information. Students:

b. locate, organize, analyze, evaluate, synthesize, and ethically use information from a variety of sources and media.

Students can use the electronic version of the "Interview Notebook Tech" (OEWS 4.3.1) when conducting their biography interviews.

Extension:

1. Challenge students to interview a teacher in the school. Students may decide to write a biography based on this in-school interview. Ask students to share the interview by creating a PowerPoint presentation, or writing an article about that teacher for the school newspaper (if applicable).

Suggested Modifications:

Assist students with special needs by helping them write the answers to the interview questions, as necessary.

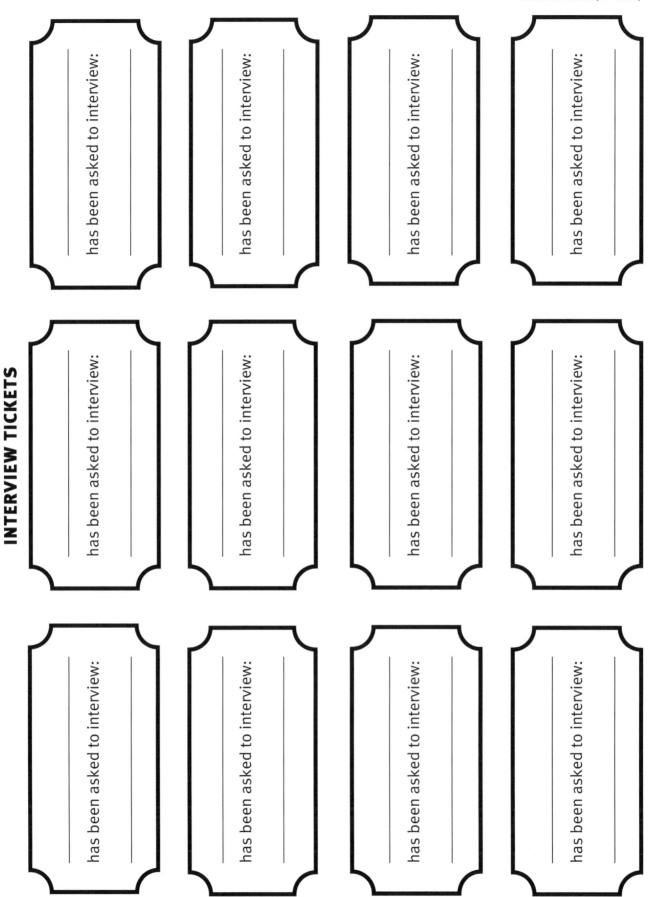

INTERVIEW TICKETS

has been asked to interview:

INTERVIEW NOTEBOOK

Interviewer's name: _____

Biography of: _____ Age: _____

1. How many people are in your family?

   (Names/Ages)_____

   _____

2. Do you have any pets?

   (Names/Kinds)_____

   _____

3. What do you enjoy doing? _____

   _____

   _____

4. What do you want to be when you grow up? Why? _____

   _____

5. Who do you admire or want to be most like?

   Why?_____

   _____

6. What is your favorite color?_____

7. What is unique about you? Share a talent, an interest, or an unusual skill.

   _____

   _____

8. Is there anyplace that you visited that you wish you could go back to or

   had an impact on you? _____

   _____

9. Where were you born?

   _____

10. When is your birthday?

    _____

11. If there is one thing that you wish you could change about the world, what

    would it be? _____

    _____

12. Have you ever been involved in any service organizations such as the Girl

    Scouts, Boy Scouts, etc? If so, what sorts of things do/did you do?

    _____

    _____

    _____

After interviewing your classmate, begin to synthesize their answers into complete sentences. Use the writing prompts below to help you get started.

How has this person's family influenced their life?

_____

_____

_____

How do you think this person's current interests will affect their future plans?

_____

_____

_____

_____

What inspires this person? Has this person had a life-changing experience?

_____

_____

_____

_____

_____

_____

STUDENT SELF-ASSESSMENT STRATEGIES

BEFORE YOU BEGIN . . .

1. Look over the interview questions. Notice that they are arranged in two sections, "Family Statistics" and "Future Plans." Think about what you hope to learn about your interviewee. How will these questions help you learn more?

_____

_____

_____

_____

2. Is there a question about their "Family Statistics" or "Future Plans" that you would like to ask that is not included? If so, write it here:

_____

_____

_____

_____

AFTER YOUR INTERVIEW . . .

1. Now that the interview is over, look over your questions and answers. Highlight the answers that you think are most important for an informative and interesting biography.

2. Read your final written biography. What could you improve? What do you like?

_____

_____

_____

_____

3. Once you have completed the biography of your classmate, exchange classmate biographies so that you are looking at the one your classmate wrote about you, and your classmate can read the one you wrote about them. Answer the classmate assessment on the back of the "Classmate Biography" (WS 4.3.2) worksheet.

3RD-GRADE LESSONS

LESSON 2: CLASSMATE BIOGRAPHIES

Coordinate! Students will use the information gathered from their student interview to write a brief biography of their classmate. *Coordinate* with the classroom teacher by offering to share the completed "Classmate Biography" (WS 4.3.2) worksheets. Sharing interesting information about students with the school community can help to form stronger relationships among the student body.

Cooperate! *Cooperate* with the classroom teacher to create a print or online biography page of a famous historical figure. Add an interesting twist by asking students what information should not be posted about this historical figure that could ruin his/her reputation. Use these kinds of conversations to discuss the ethics involved in posting online information. This may be student's first exposure to this type of conversation.

Lesson Plan

Integrated Goals:

Language Arts

Standard 12. Students use spoken, written, and visual language to accomplish their own purposes (e.g., for learning, enjoyment, persuasion, and the exchange of information).

Library Media

AASL 21st Century Standards

> **Standard 3:** Share knowledge and participate ethically and productively as members of our democratic society.

Essential Questions:

> How can biographies give you greater insights about a famous person who has made an important contribution to society?
> How can reading biographies enrich our own lives?

Desired Understandings:

Students will understand:

> What information can be found in a biography by participating in their own biographical interview.
> How biographies can enrich the lives of those who read them.

Integrated Objectives:

- Students will conduct an interview and write a simple biography about a classmate.

Time Required:

45 minutes

Provided Materials:

- "Interview Notebook" (WS 4.3.1)—completed from previous lesson
- "Classmate Biography" (WS 4.3.2)—one per student
- "Student Self-Assessment Strategy" (WS 4.3.3)—one per student partially completed from the previous lesson

Materials You Will Need to Obtain:

- Computer
- Projection device
- Pencils
- Biography books of a wide variety displayed for the class to view and check out
- Access to the following Web site: http://www.readingrockets.org/books/interviews/
- Books written by the author you choose to highlight (see information below)

Prior to the Lesson:

Go to the Reading Rockets Web site, http://www.readingrockets.org/books/interviews/. Choose an author that you think your students will know. Preview the interview transcript. The transcripts contain the answers to unheard interview questions on the video. Create a question for the answer the author gave on the video. For example, Eric Rohmann begins his interview by saying his name and what he does for a living. He goes on to explain what he writes about. A good interview question would be, "Eric, tell us a little bit about yourself and what kinds of things you write about." Preview a part of an interview with your chosen author and create the question.

Lesson Procedures:

Engagement:

1. Show students the portion of the author's interview that you planned to show from above. Set the interview up by telling students the kinds of books this author has written. Showcase a few in front of the class. Then, ask the author your question. Play the portion of the video that answers your question. Tell students that this kind of interview question and answer session can be the basis for the beginning of a biography because it is important to learn information about a person before beginning to write a biography about them.

Activity:

2. Instruct students to sit with their same partner from the previous class and redistribute the "Interview Notebooks" (WS 4.3.1) and the "Student Self-Assessment Strategy" (WS 4.3.3).

3. Instruct students to synthesize their classmate's responses into complete sentences on page three of their notebooks. Explain that this will help students as they create their final biography of their classmate.
4. Allow students time to complete the notebooks.
5. Display the "Classmate Biography" (WS 4.3.2) worksheet for students to see. Demonstrate how to complete the biography by taking information from the "Interview Notebook" (WS 4.3.1) and placing it in the "Classmate Biography" (WS 4.3.2) worksheet. Be sure and point out that there is a space for a picture of the student being interviewed. Also, some of the blank spaces will require the students to think about what is required for the space and then rephrase the answer from their "Interview Notebook" (WS 4.3.1) to properly fit and make sense in the "Classmate Biography" (WS 4.3.2) worksheet.
6. Explain to students that many people choose to post biographical information about themselves on Web sites. This will be an opportune time to explain the importance of posting information in a responsible manner.

Transition:

7. Distribute the "Classmate Biography" (WS 4.3.2) worksheets for students to complete.

Activity:

8. Give students time to complete the biographies of their classmates. This may take an additional class period depending upon your students.

Embedded AASL Skills Indicator: ___.___.___: _____

_____

Embedded AASL Self-Assessment Strategies: ___.___.___: _____

_____

9. Once students have complete their "Classmate Biography" (WS 4.3.2), they should exchange the biography with the classmate it is about. The classmate should make comments and provide feedback in the classmate assessment portion on the back of the "Classmate Biography" (WS 4.3.2).

Embedded AASL Responsibilities Indicator: ___.___.___: _____

_____

10. After students have completed their "Classmate Biography" (WS 4.3.2) worksheet, invite them to read a biography on display while they wait for others to finish.
11. Once everyone has completed their "Classmate Biography" (WS 4.3.2) worksheet, ask for student volunteers to share their work with the class.

Closure:

12. Point out the biography section of the media center to the class and encourage students to read stories about the lives of famous people.
13. Ask students if they think it would be easier or more difficult if they wrote their own autobiography as opposed to writing the biography of another person and explain why.

Evidence of Understanding:

Collect and grade the "Classmate Biography" (WS 4.3.2) worksheets and the "Interview Notebooks" (WS 4.3.1) for neatness, accuracy of information, and completeness. Think about creating a biography bulletin board to showcase student work. Consider designing the bulletin board to resemble online biography spaces.

Technology Integration:

Technology

NETS-S

3. Research and Information Fluency

Students apply digital tools to gather, evaluate, and use information. Students:

  b. locate, organize, analyze, evaluate, synthesize, and ethically use information from a variety of sources and media.

   Option 1: Students can complete the electronic version of the "Classmate Biography" (OEWS 4.3.2) instead of the print version.

   Option 2: Students can explore famous people and learn more about their lives on this BBC site: http://www.bbc.co.uk/schools/famouspeople/flash/index.shtml.

Extension:

1. Encourage students to interview a person outside of the school building. Students may wish to interview a nearby author, parent, local celebrity, community member, or relative via the telephone or video conference. Assist students with their interview questions. Challenge students to share their interview during morning announcements, or write an article or brief biography summary for the school newspaper or school Web site.

Suggested Modifications:

You may wish to help some students by offering sentence starters for their biographies. In addition, it may be necessary to assist students by offering to scribe for them.

CLASSMATE BIOGRAPHY

Biography of a Classmate

Place photo here.

Name: _____

Age: _____

Boy: ☐   Girl: ☐

City: _____

State: _____

Birthday: _____

You won't believe this!

Family Statistics:

Number of people in their family _____

Names/Ages:

_____

_____

Kinds of pets he/she owns and their names: _____

_____

Their birthplace:

_____

Future Plans:

When they grow up:

Inspirations/ Life-changing moment:

Classmate Assessment

Did your classmate write an accurate biography about you? Explain your answer.

_____

_____

_____

_____

Do you have any suggestions for improvement? What are they?

_____

_____

_____

_____

Working in Collaboration

Collaborate! True collaboration requires both the library media specialist and the classroom teacher to share in the design of integrated instruction. Collaboration provides you with an excellent opportunity to design inquiry-based learning activities. Here are some ideas for collaborating with the classroom teachers.

3rd Grade: Language Arts

Essential Question: How can learning about the lives of others change the way I see things?

- Have students read a biography about someone who has made a significant contribution to our democratic society. Students can share the significant contribution made by the person they read about. Students could write about what life as we know it would be like if the person they read about had never been born.

For further information, please visit
www.destinationcollaboration.com

4TH-GRADE LESSONS

LESSON 1: FAMOUS AMERICAN BIOGRAPHIES

Coordinate! *Coordinate* with the classroom teacher by offering to teach this lesson when the classroom teacher is teaching students about biographies. Offer to bring a diverse selection of biography books to the classroom for the students to use during independent reading activities. Students may discover new interests as they read about the accomplishments of others.

Cooperate! Discuss some of the famous people students may be learning about in their classroom. *Cooperate* with the classroom teacher by using these famous people as choices for students to make their game about. The classroom teacher can then use the completed guessing games to reinforce classroom topics.

Lesson Plan

Integrated Goals:

Language Arts

Standard 8. Students use a variety of technological and information resources (e.g., libraries, databases, computer networks, video) to gather and synthesize information and to create and communicate knowledge.

Technology

NETS-S

3. Research and Information Fluency

Students apply digital tools to gather, evaluate, and use information. Students:

b. locate, organize, analyze, evaluate, synthesize, and ethically use information from a variety of sources and media.

Library Media

AASL 21st Century Standards

> **Standard 1:** Inquire, think critically, and gain knowledge.
> **Standard 4:** Pursue personal and aesthetic growth.

Essential Questions:

> How can reading multiple resources about a famous person and their important contributions to society give you more complete insight into their life?
> How can reading biographies enrich our own lives?

Desired Understandings:

Students will understand:

How reading about the lives of others can inspire us in our own lives.
The importance of using multiple resources to answer an information need.

Integrated Objectives:

- Students will research a famous American in order to create a game about why they are/were important.

Time Required:

45 minutes

Provided Materials:

- "Biography Guessing Game" (MN 4.4.1)
- "Famous Americans" (RS 4.4.1)
- "Name Game Planning Sheet" (WS 4.4.1)—one per student printed back to back and folded like a booklet

Materials You Will Need to Obtain:

- Projection device
- Pencils
- Computers available for student use with access to Internet and databases
- Set of encyclopedias
- Biography books of famous Americans
- Computer

Prior to the Lesson:

Print the "Biography Guessing Game" (MN 4.4.1) onto cardstock and cut out the pieces, then tape them on the board or place them on a pocket chart facedown and in the correct order.

Lesson Procedures:

Engagement:

1. Tell students that they will play a guessing game to figure out which famous person you have featured on the board. Explain that you will turn over a clue on the board and if students think they know the famous person you are describing, they should raise their hand.
2. Call on a few students to volunteer their ideas. Continue game play until all but the last card has been uncovered. Ask for one more student response before uncovering the answer of "Milton Bradley."

Activity:

3. Tell students that like Milton Bradley, they will be creating a game. In order to make their game, they must first each research the biography of a famous American.
4. Ask students to recall the definition of biography.

5. Tell students that they will be using skills they have learned in previous lessons to help them locate their information (text features and how to use the public access catalog). Ask students to share places to look for information about famous Americans. List their suggestions on the board.

6. Explain to students that they will be using many resources to locate information about the famous American they are assigned. They will use preselected Internet Web sites, biography and autobiography books, online databases, and the encyclopedia to retrieve their information.

7. Tell students that because this is not a book report where they would be expected to read an entire book and then later extract and interpret the information they find, they will need to use text features to assist them in locating information to complete their "Name Game Planning Sheet" (WS 4.4.1).

Embedded AASL Dispositions in Action Indicator: ___.___.___: _____

_____

8. Students should use the index and table of contents to easily locate specific information about their famous American. For example, remind students that they will most likely be able to find out their person's date of birth or information about their childhood in a chapter entitled "Early Years." Remind students that they may need to consult multiple resources because they may not find all of the information they need from just one.

Embedded AASL Responsibilities Indicator: ___.___.___: _____

_____

9. Because students are using multiple resources, remind them how important it will be for them to cite where they found their information. Show students the back of the "Name Game Planning Sheet" (WS 4.4.1) so they know where to cite the resources they use.

Transition:

10. Distribute the "Name Game Planning Sheet" (WS 4.4.1).
11. Tell students that the front of their booklet says "Top Secret" because students are not to share the information they learn about their person with other students in the class, or in other classes for that matter. The game will be a lot more fun if they don't share their facts.

Activity:

Embedded AASL Dispositions in Action Indicator: ___.___.___: _____

_____

12. Give students access to the computers to locate books and information to complete their "Name Game Planning Sheet" (WS 4.4.1).

Embedded AASL Skills Indicator: ___.___.___: _____

_____

13. Once students have located their necessary resources, allow students time to take notes and complete the "Name Game Planning Sheet" (WS 4.4.1).
14. Walk around the room to make yourself available should students require assistance.

Embedded AASL Self-Assessment Strategies: ___.___.___: _____

_____

15. Instruct students to monitor their own progress as they use various resources to gather the information they need to complete their "Name Game Planning Sheet" (WS 4.4.1). If the sources they are using do not satisfy the needs of the assignment, they should look for a different resource to use.

Closure:

16. Ask students to share which resources they found to be the most helpful for this project.

Embedded AASL Skills Indicator: ___.___.___: _____

_____

17. Have students share how the biography of the person whom they researched may have changed or validated their way of thinking about a topic.
18. Collect the "Name Game Planning Sheet" (WS 4.4.1).

Evidence of Understanding:

Collect and check to see that students were able to successfully locate information to complete most of their "Name Game Planning Sheet" (WS 4.4.1).

Enrichment Using Technology:

1. Students can play the "Who Is That?" game on Funbrain in which they try to guess the famous American by looking at a picture and several clues about the person's life (http://www.funbrain.com/who/index.html).

> **DISCUSSION OPPORTUNITY**
>
> After completing this lesson, ask students to think about the interests of the famous people they read about. How did learning about these people affect the way students see themselves in the future?

Extension:

1. Select a chapter from the book *Toys!: Amazing Stories Behind Some Great Inventions* by Don L. Wulffson (New York: Henry Holt, 2000) to read to the class. Students will connect the toys discussed in the book to the famous people who created them.

Suggested Modifications:

Assist students with special needs with extracting information from the biography resources. Assign these students with famous American's from the suggested Web sites. The Web sites are good resources for students to easily locate the necessary facts they need for their "Name Game Planning Sheet" (WS 4.4.1).

BIOGRAPHY GUESSING GAME

Directions for use: Print on cardstock and laminate (if you wish to use from year to year). Place the cards on the board face down, and in the order they are numbered for most effective use/game play.

Born in Vienna, Maine
November 8, 1836

1.

Died May 30, 1911

2.

Published magazines about the education of kindergarten children

3.

Inducted into the National Toy Hall of Fame in 2004

4.

Many consider him the founding father of the game industry in North America.

5.

The first game he created was called the Checkered Game of Life—now known as the Game of Life.

6.

From *Destination Collaboration 2: A Complete Reference Focused Curriculum Guidebook to Educate 21st Century Learners in Grades 3–5* by

182 Danielle N. DuPuis and Lori M. Carter. Santa Barbara, CA: Libraries Unlimited. Copyright © 2011.

The company that he founded is still around today. Responsible for making games such as Yahtzee; Connect Four; Hungry, Hungry Hippos; and Battleship, the company is now owned by Hasbro.

7.

Who is this famous American?
Milton Bradley

8.

FAMOUS AMERICANS

Harriet Tubman

George Washington Carver

Noah Webster

Thomas Paine

Rachel Carson

Robert E. Lee

Helen Keller

Susan B. Anthony

Amelia Earhart

Meriwether Lewis

William Clark

Thomas Alva Edison

Harry Houdini

Buffalo Bill Cody

Pocahontas

George S. Patton Jr.

John Phillip Sousa

Duke Ellington

Martin Luther King Jr.

Theodore Roosevelt

John Quincy Adams

Mark Twain

Langston Hughes

Frank Lloyd Wright

Dorothea Lange

Top Secret

GUESS THE NAME GAME PLANNING SHEET

Research conducted by: _____

NAME GAME PLANNING SHEET

Works Cited (places I looked and found my information)

Name of famous American: _____

Accomplishments: _____
_____
_____

Date they were born: _____

Place of birth: _____

Date they died (if applicable): _____

How did this person affect the lives of others?: _____
_____
_____

Interesting facts about their childhood that may relate to why they are famous: _____
_____
_____
_____
_____

Why they are famous: _____
_____

Famous quote (if any): _____
_____
_____

4TH-GRADE LESSONS

LESSON 2: NAME OF THE GAME

 **Coordinate!** Inform teachers about this lesson. Once the lesson is complete, *coordinate* by sharing the completed "Name Game" with the classroom teacher. He or she may wish to play the game with their students outside of the media classroom. Consider sharing online biography resources with the classroom teacher to use for an upcoming project.

Cooperate! *Cooperate* with the classroom teacher by sharing the Web site used in the engagement activity of this lesson (http://www.biography.com/bio4kids/factsoflives/index.jsp). This Web site will provide teachers with many resources to use in classroom activities involving biographies. Study guides are offered with each video found in the teacher section of the Web site. Offer to extend biography lessons in the classroom by looking at the resources featured on the Web site and thinking of ways to further *cooperate*.

Lesson Plan

Integrated Goals:

Language Arts

Standard 8. Students use a variety of technological and information resources (e.g., libraries, databases, computer networks, video) to gather and synthesize information and to create and communicate knowledge.

Standard 12. Students use spoken, written, and visual language to accomplish their own purposes (e.g., for learning, enjoyment, persuasion, and the exchange of information).

Technology

NETS-S

3. Research and Information Fluency

Students apply digital tools to gather, evaluate, and use information. Students:

b. locate, organize, analyze, evaluate, synthesize, and ethically use information from a variety of sources and media.

Library Media

AASL 21st Century Standards

   Standard 3: Share knowledge and participate ethically and productively as members of our democratic society.

Essential Questions:

How can reading multiple resources about a famous person and their important contributions to society give you greater insights about their life?

How can reading biographies enrich our own lives?

CLASSROOM CONNECTION

Ask the classroom teacher what subject students are currently learning about in the classroom. Select biographies relating to these subjects for students to research for this project.

Desired Understandings:

Students will understand:

How reading about the lives of others can inspire us in our own lives.
The importance of using multiple resources to answer an information need.

Integrated Objectives:

- Students will research a famous American in order to create a game about why they are/were important.

Time Required:

45 minutes

Provided Materials:

- "Name Game Planning Sheet" (WS 4.4.1)—completed from previous lesson
- "Name Game Cards" (WS 4.4.2)
- "Name Game Sample" (RS 4.4.2)
- "Name Game Directions" (RS 4.4.3)

Materials You Will Need to Obtain:

- Computer
- Projection device
- Pencils
- Scissors
- Computers available for student use with access to Internet and databases
- Set of encyclopedias
- Biography books of famous Americans
- Optional—recipe box or shoe box, colored paper, glue, and colored pencils for students to use for decorating a container to hold the completed "Name Game"

Lesson Procedures:

Engagement:

1. Display the Web site http://www.biography.com/bio4kids/factsoflives/index.jsp. Take the quiz with the class to see what they know. Remind students that today they will be finishing their "Name Game" and will have an opportunity to play it with the class.

Activity:

2. Redistribute the "Name Game Planning Sheet" (WS 4.4.1). Allow students time to complete the worksheet.

3. Display the "Name Game Sample" (RS 4.4.2) for students to see. Using Milton Bradley as an example, demonstrate the proper way to fill this out.

Embedded AASL Skills Indicator: ___.___.___: _____

_____

4. Distribute the "Name Game Cards" (WS 4.4.2) and give students time to complete.
5. After students have neatly completed their "Name Game Card" (WS 4.4.2), instruct students to cut out their card and bring it to the front of the room.
6. Students that finish early can work on designing a box or container to store "The Name Game."

Transition:

7. Once everyone has completed their "Name Game Card" (WS 4.4.2), place students into four teams.

Activity:

8. Shuffle the collected "Name Game Cards" (WS 4.4.2).
9. Use the "Name Game Directions" (RS 4.4.3) to assist you in explaining the rules of "The Name Game." Also tell students to pay close attention during the game—they will be asked to share something they learned at the end of the class.

Embedded AASL Dispositions in Action Indicator: ___.___.___: _____

_____

Embedded AASL Responsibilities Indicator: ___.___.___: _____

_____

10. Play the name game until it is time for the class to come to an end.

Closure:

11. Congratulate the class on their hard work.

Embedded AASL Self-Assessment Strategies: ___.___.___: _____

_____

12. Ask students to share something they learned today about a famous American aside from the one they researched.

13. Be sure and point out your biography section to the class and encourage students to read stories about the lives of other famous people.
14. Allow the team with the most points to line up first.

Evidence of Understanding:

Collect and grade the "Name Game Cards" (WS 4.4.2) for neatness, accuracy of information, and completeness.

Technology Integration:

Technology

NETS-S

6. Technology operations and concepts

Students demonstrate a sound understanding of technology concepts, systems, and operations. Students:

a. understand and use technology systems.
 1. Provide students with a computer and access to the electronic version of the "Name Game Cards Tech" (OEWS 4.4.2). Completing these cards electronically and printing them out will provide your game with a more professional look and feel. You may even wish to print them on cardstock and consider laminating them to guarantee many more uses for years to come.

Extension:

1. Have students use the public access catalog to locate more names of famous Americans that can be used for future classes. You may also wish to encourage students to locate information about someone that interests them from this century. They could even create a "Famous Americans of the 21st Century Game."

Suggested Modifications:

Be sure to group students heterogeneously in order to create groups with students of mixed ability levels.

NAME GAME CARDS

The Name Game

5._____

4._____

3._____

2._____

1._____

Answer:_____

The Name Game

5._____

4._____

3._____

2._____

1._____

Answer:_____

The Name Game

5._____

4._____

3._____

2._____

1._____

Answer:_____

The Name Game

5._____

4._____

3._____

2._____

1._____

Answer:_____

The Name Game

5._____

4._____

3._____

2._____

1._____

Answer:_____

The Name Game

5._____

4._____

3._____

2._____

1._____

Answer:_____

NAME GAME SAMPLE

Directions: Type each of your clues into the name game card below. Don't forget to type in your answer (the name of your famous American).

THE NAME GAME

5. Born November 18, 1836, in Vienna, Maine.

4. Supported early childhood education as well as art programs.

3. Owned a lithography business in Massachusetts.

2. Attended Harvard's Lawrence Scientific School.

1. Created a board game called the Checkered Game of Life. He was the founder of a game company that is now owned by Hasbro.

   Answer: Milton Bradley

NAME GAME DIRECTIONS

HOW TO PLAY THE "NAME GAME"

Directions:

1. Place students into four teams, and write the name of each team on the board.

2. Shuffle the name game cards.

3. Randomly select a card.

4. Read the first fact about the person out loud. If a team thinks they know the answer, they can raise their hand. If they give the answer and it is incorrect, no points are awarded and the team will be disqualified from answering again on this name game card. Play then continues for the remaining teams. The facts on the cards are numbered backwards for a reason. If a team guesses correctly after only the first statement next to number 5, their team is then awarded 5 points. If after the first statement is read and none of the teams know the answer, read the second statement (worth 4 points) and so on until all the statements have been read. However long it takes for a team to guess the correct answer will determine the number of points they earn for their team. If they need all five statements in order to guess the answer, they will earn only 1 point.

5. Record the points on the board.

6. Select a new card and continue game play until all the cards have been used.

7. The team with the most points is the winner.

Working in Collaboration

Collaborate! True collaboration requires both the library media specialist and the classroom teacher to share in the design of integrated instruction. Collaboration provides you with an excellent opportunity to design inquiry-based learning activities. Here are some ideas for collaborating with the classroom teachers.

4th Grade: Science, Social Studies

Essential Question: How have the contributions of others helped to advance our society?

- Select biographies about famous people who have made a significant contribution in the science or social studies field. Students can contribute to a wiki or online learning space and collaboratively discuss how the people they read about have helped advance our society. Students can share their ideas for how society may be further changed by this person's contribution(s). Students may also discuss how current events have further impacted this person's contribution. For example: Louis Pasteur created the rabies vaccine, which is still in use today.

> For further information, please visit
> www.destinationcollaboration.com

5TH-GRADE LESSONS

LESSON 1: BIOGRAPHY RÉSUMÉ

Coordinate! Holding a career day at your school is a great way for students to see what types of jobs may be available. Career day guests can discuss the importance of résumés and how they were able to assist them in getting a good job. *Coordinate* with the classroom teacher by preparing a display of the completed student résumés to share with the guests at your school on career day.

Cooperate! Once students have completed their biography résumés, *cooperate* with the classroom teacher to create a list of interview questions that could be asked of the students in the class. Students can pretend to be the person they researched, and answer the interview questions from the perspective of that person.

Lesson Plan

Integrated Goals:

Language Arts

Standard 2. Students read a wide range of literature from many periods in many genres to build an understanding of the many dimensions (e.g. philosophical, ethical, aesthetic) of human experience.

Standard 8. Students use a variety of technological and information resources (e.g., libraries, databases, computer networks, video) to gather and synthesize information and to create and communicate knowledge.

History

Standards in Historical Thinking

Standard 2: Grades 5–12 The student comprehends a variety of historical sources. Therefore, the student is able to:

E. Read historical narratives imaginatively.

Library Media

AASL 21st Century Standards

Standard 1: Inquire, think critically, and gain knowledge.
Standard 2: Draw conclusions, make informed decisions, apply knowledge to new situations, and create new knowledge.

Essential Questions:

How does the use of multiple resources and text features help you locate the information necessary to answer and information need?

How does creating a résumé help you understand the importance of a person's career?

Desired Understandings:

Students will understand:

The importance of using multiple resources when answering a question.

How a résumé highlights the important parts of a person's career.

Integrated Objectives:

- Students will research a famous person and create a current job résumé for that person.
- Students will use multiple resources to locate necessary information.
- Students will create a résumé for their historical person in order for them to apply for a job that may be available today.

Time Required:

45 minutes

Provided Materials:

- "Biography Résumé" (WS 4.5.1)
- "Biography Résumé Sample" (ORS 4.5.1)

Materials You Will Need to Obtain:

- Computer
- Projection device
- Pencils
- Classified section of your local newspaper
- Computers available for student use with access to Internet and databases
- Set of encyclopedias
- Biography books

Prior to the Lesson:

Circle a variety of ads from the classified section of your local newspaper that students may find of interest.

Lesson Procedures:

Engagement:

1. Pretend that you are reading the classified section as students come into the classroom. Say things like "Ooh! This sounds neat!" or "Oh, I can do that!" or perhaps "This would be the perfect job for me!" Inform students that you are looking at the classified section of the newspaper. Ask students if they know what that means.
2. Explain that many companies advertise in the paper and on the Internet and sometimes even on the radio or on television commercials if they have a job opening that needs to be filled.

3. Read a few of the job descriptions for students to hear. Ask students what the next step would be for someone who saw a job advertised that they would like to have?

Activity:

4. Tell students that in order to get a good job, they need to write a good résumé. A résumé can be like an advertisement in the way that you will be promoting all the good things about yourself to a potential employer.

5. Tell students to pretend for a minute that a famous person such as Benjamin Franklin was alive today and needed to apply for a job. What do you think he would write on his résumé? Obviously he couldn't put items such as "works well with computers" because computers were far from being invented at the time he was alive. However, he could put something like "innovative thinker, good at inventing, and so forth."

6. Explain that students will choose a historical famous person, research them, and write a résumé for them. Depending on the job for which they want to apply, they may wish to highlight different skills. Also, students will want to pick a job that would be appropriate for their person. For example, if students research a person who is mentioned as having poor athletic ability, the student would not want to create a résumé for this person to apply to be a quarterback for the Dallas Cowboys.

Embedded AASL Skills Indicator: ___.___.___: _____

7. Tell students that they will be using skills they have learned in previous lessons to help them locate their information (text features and how to use the public access catalog). Ask students to share places to look for information about famous people. List their suggestions on the board.

8. Explain to students that they will be using many resources to locate information about famous people. They will use biography and autobiography books, online databases, and the encyclopedia to retrieve their information.

9. Tell students that because this is not a book report where they would be expected to read an entire book and then later extract and interpret the information they find, they will need to use text features to assist them in locating information to complete their "Biography Résumé" (WS 4.5.1).

10. Students should use the index and table of contents to easily locate specific information about their famous person. For example, remind students that they will most likely be able to find out what was significant about their person's life in a chapter entitled "Making a Big Change."

Embedded AASL Skills Indicator: ___.___.___: _____

11. Ask students to think of historical famous people. Write their suggestions on the board until there are enough ideas for each student in the class to select one.
12. Display the "Biography Résumé Sample" (ORS 4.5.1). Show students how the information needs to be displayed in their résumé.

Transition:

13. Distribute the "Biography Résumé" (WS 4.5.1).

Activity:

14. Instruct students to record the name of the person they will be researching on the top of their paper.

Embedded AASL Skills Indicator: ___.___.___: _____

_____

15. Give students access to the computers to locate books and information to complete their "Biography Résumé" (WS 4.5.1).

Embedded AASL Dispositions in Action Indicator: ___.___.___: _____

_____

16. Encourage students to keep looking for information if they have difficulties locating appropriate information for this task. Assist them, as necessary, in locating appropriate resources.

Embedded AASL Self-Assessment Strategies: ___.___.___: _____

_____

17. Once students have located their necessary resources, allow students time to complete the "Biography Résumé" (WS 4.5.1). Encourage students to ask for help if needed.
18. Walk around the room to make yourself available should students require assistance.

Embedded AASL Dispositions in Action Indicator: ___.___.___: _____

_____

19. If you can determine that some students are displaying confidence in their information search and it is resulting in locating appropriate information, ask these students to share their thinking with the rest of the class.

Closure:

20. Ask students to share which resources they found to be the most helpful for this project.

Embedded AASL Responsibilities Indicator: ___.___.___: _____

---

21. Ask students how writing the résumé for their historical person helped them understand the importance of their career.
22. Collect the "Biography Résumé" (WS 4.5.1).
23. Tell students that they may wish to dress in a professional manner for next week's lesson. Explain that a job scout will be attending next week's class and will be conducting interviews of potential candidates for some open job positions.

Evidence of Understanding:

Collect and check to see that students were able to successfully locate information to complete most of their "Biography Résumé" (WS 4.5.1).

Technology Integration:

Technology

NETS-S

6. Technology Operations and Concepts

Students demonstrate a sound understanding of technology concepts, systems, and operations. Students:

a. understand and use technology systems.
   1. Provide students with a computer and access to "Biography Résumé Tech" (OEWS 4.5.1). Students can type the answers directly into the document. Students can easily adjust the font and spacing they will need for each section with this electronic version.

Extension:

1. Share a few of the job descriptions from the book *Archers, Alchemists and 98 Other Medieval Jobs You Might Have Loved Or Loathed* by Priscilla Galloway (Buffalo, NY: Annick Press, 2003). Students might be inspired to create a classified ad for one of the jobs in this particular time period.

Suggested Modifications:

Assist students with special needs in locating biography books at their reading level. This will make extracting necessary information much easier.

BIOGRAPHY RÉSUMÉ

Name: _____

Résumé prepared by: _____

Objective	
Why do you want this position?	
Education	
Work Experience	
Other Qualifications	
References	

5TH-GRADE LESSONS

LESSON 2: GETTING A JOB

Coordinate! There may be student jobs available at your school. For example: media helpers, safeties, students who assist with gathering and distributing supplies, and so forth. *Coordinate* with the classroom teacher to assist students in building their own personal résumé, which can include job experience gained during the school year as students participate in the aforementioned job activities.

Cooperate! *Cooperate* with the classroom teacher by sharing the link to the "My First Résumé" Web site listed in the "Enrichment Using Technology" section of this lesson. Offer to bring in a selection of books about various jobs to the classroom for students to explore and learn about what career they may be interested in pursuing in the future and why. Students should consult the résumé they completed to assist them in making an appropriate choice.

Lesson Plan

Integrated Goals:

Standard 8. Students use a variety of technological and information resources (e.g., libraries, databases, computer networks, video) to gather and synthesize information and to create and communicate knowledge.

Standard 12. Students use spoken, written, and visual language to accomplish their own purposes (e.g., for learning, enjoyment, persuasion, and the exchange of information).

Library Media

AASL 21st Century Standards

> **Standard 3:** Share knowledge and participate ethically and productively as members of our democratic society.

Essential Questions:

> How does creating a résumé help you understand the importance of a person's career?
> How would information you include in your own résumé help you to share your skills and qualifications when looking for a job?

Desired Understandings:

Students will understand:

> How a résumé highlights the important parts of person's career.
> How a résumé is connected to showing a potential employer you have the right skills for the job.

Integrated Objectives:

- Students will research a famous historical person and create a current job résumé for that person.
- Students will participate in an interview; they will take on the persona of the famous person they researched to answer interview questions.

Time Required:

45 minutes

Provided Materials:

- "Biography Résumé" (WS 4.5.1)—completed from previous class
- "Interview Questions" (RS 4.5.1)
- "Biography Grading Sheet" (RS 4.5.3)—one half sheet per student

Materials You Will Need to Obtain:

- Computer
- Projection device
- Pencils
- Scissors
- Computers available for student use with access to Internet and databases
- Set of encyclopedias
- Biography books of famous Americans

Lesson Procedures

Engagement:

1. Ask students what they would like to be when they grow up. Write down their ideas on the board.
2. Ask students how they might go about getting these sorts of jobs (e.g., participate in activities that relate to the job they want to do, gain job skills through a work skills program or by going to college, writing a good résumé, going on an interview, etc.).

Embedded AASL Responsibilities Indicator: ___.___.___: _____

3. Tell students that once their résumé has been written, the next step will be to go through an interview.

Activity:

4. Redistribute the "Biography Résumé." (WS 4.5.1). Allow students time to complete the worksheet.
5. Tell students that the rest of the class time will be used to interview potential job candidates (the students in the class). Student's jobs will be to become the person they researched and answer the questions to the best of their ability from the perspective and point of view of the person they researched.

Transition:

Embedded AASL Dispositions in Action Indicator: ___.___.___: _____

_____

6. Once everyone has completed their "Biography Résumé" (WS 4.5.1), inform students that you will be selecting students for their interviews based on when they (the person they researched) were born, beginning with the most recent.

Activity:

7. Tell students that it is now time for the interviews to begin.
8. Choose a student whose person they researched was born in the 1900s.

Embedded AASL Skills Indicator: ___.___.___: _____

_____

9. Have this student come to the front of the room for their interview. Explain that you will ask the candidate a series of questions, and they will be scored on their effort and quality of their answers.
10. Read the "Interview Questions" (RS 4.5.1) and score the student using the "Biography Grading Sheet" (RS 4.5.3). Continue until all the students in the class have had an opportunity to interview.

Closure:

Embedded AASL Self-Assessment Strategies: ___.___.___: _____

_____

11. Ask students to assess their résumé by thinking about their ability to answer questions during the interview process. If they felt that the interview was "easy," ask them to explain why they believe this to be true. If they felt that the interview was "difficult," ask them to explain why their résumé did not help them with the interview. Discuss what they would do differently in the future.
12. Congratulate the class on their hard work.
13. Explain that while you only had one opening, that you will have to find a job for all of the students since they did such a great job. You'll check with your boss to see if there can be extra funding to create more positions.

Evidence of Understanding:

Collect and grade the "Biography Résumés" (WS 4.5.1) for neatness, accuracy of information, creativity, and completeness.

Enrichment Using Technology:

1. Have students go to the following Web site: http://www.careerkids.com/1152x864/resume.html. Here, they can create their own résumé, and print it out to share with the class, school, or their family.

Extension:

1. Provide students with a blank copy of the "Biography Résumé" (WS 4.5.1). Students can write a résumé for one of their favorite characters from a story they read to help promote and "book talk" the title to other students in the school.

Suggested Modifications:

For students with difficulties memorizing or remembering, allow them to use their résumé for assistance as they answer their questions.

INTERVIEW QUESTIONS

Directions: Ask the students the five questions below. As they answer, use the "Biography Grading Sheet" to record their points. The maximum amount of points that can be earned is 12. Use the grading rubric below as well as the point suggestions next to each question to assist you in completing the "Biography Grading Sheet."

1. Please state your name. (1 point)

2. For what position are you applying? (1 point)

3. What qualities do you have that qualify you for this position? (use the rubric below to grade this question)

4. What work experience do you have that may prepare you for taking this position? (use the rubric below to grade this question)

5. List three words to describe yourself. (up to 2 points)

Grading Rubric

4 Points	3 Points	2 Points	1 Point
Applicant was able to clearly and concisely answer the question. Three or more examples were cited.	Applicant was able to clearly answer the question. Two examples were cited.	Applicant was able to answer the question with little hesitation. Only one example was cited.	Applicant had a difficult time answering the question. Examples were cited poorly or not at all.

BIOGRAPHY GRADING SHEET

Student name: _____

Famous person researched: _____

Question	Possible Points	Points Earned	Comments
State your name.	1		
For what position are you applying?	1		
What qualities do you have that qualify you for this position?	4		
What work experience do you have that may prepare you for taking this position?	4		
List three words to describe yourself.	2		
	12		

- -

Student name: _____

Famous person researched: _____

Question	Possible Points	Points Earned	Comments
State your name.	1		
For what position are you applying?	1		
What qualities do you have that qualify you for this position?	4		
What work experience do you have that may prepare you for taking this position?	4		
List three words to describe yourself.	2		
	12		

Working in Collaboration

Collaborate! True collaboration requires both the library media specialist and the classroom teacher to share in the design of integrated instruction. Collaboration provides you with an excellent opportunity to design inquiry-based learning activities. Here are some ideas for collaborating with the classroom teachers.

5th Grade: Social Studies

Essential Question: How can a résumé help me to get into a college, trade school, or get a job?

- Students can record their strengths and skills and then research different jobs to figure out what they would like to do in the future. Once they have established a career path, students can assess what skills and experiences are necessary in order to accomplish their goal. Students can create a plan of action for achieving success.

For further information, please visit
www.destinationcollaboration.com

Bibliography

Work Cited

Waldstreicher, David. "Benjamin Franklin." *World Book. World Book Online Reference Center.* 2008. Web. 30 Nov. 2008. <http://www.worldbookonline.com//?id=ar209260>.

Suggested Book Resources

Galloway, Priscilla. *Archers, Alchemists, and 98 Other Medieval Jobs You Might Have Loved or Loathed.* Buffalo: Annick Press, 2003. Print.

Levstik, Linda S., and Keith C. Barton. *Doing History: Investigating with Children in Elementary and Middle Schools.* Philadelphia: Lawrence Erlbaum Associates, 2001. 40. Print.

Miller, Raymond H. *Inventors and Creators- Milton Bradley.* Detroit: KidHaven Press, 2005. Print.

Wulffson, Don L. *Toys!: Amazing Stories Behind Some Great Inventions.* New York: H. Holt, 2000. Print.

Suggested Web Resources

"The Achiever Gallery." *Academy of Achievement.* 2008. Web. 14 Dec. 2008. <http://www.achievement.org/autodoc/pagegen/galleryachieve.html>.

"Betcha Didn't Know Videos." *Bio4Kids.* 2008. Web. 30 Nov. 2008. <http://www.biography.com/kids/kids-video.jsp>.

"The Facts of Lives Challenge." *Bio4Kids.* 2008. Web. 29 Nov. 2008. <http://www.biography.com/kids/factsoflives/.jsp>.

"Famous People." *BBC Schools.* Web. 30 Nov. 2008. <http://www.bbc.co.uk/schools/famouspeople/flash/index.shtml>.

"Meet Amazing Americans." *America's Story From America's Library.* 2000. Web. 26 Nov. 2008. <http://www.americaslibrary.gov/cgi-bin/page.cgi/aa>.

"Multimedia Biographies." *Houghton Mifflin Harcourt School Publishers.* Web. 26 Nov. 2008. <http://www.harcourtschool.com/activity/biographies/>.

"My First Résumé." *CareerKids.* 2008. Web. 30 Nov. 2008. <http://www.careerkids.com/1152x864/resume.html>.

"Video Interviews." *Reading Rockets.* 2008. Web. 14 Dec. 2008. <http://www.readingrockets.org/books/interviews/>.

"Who is That?" *Funbrain.* 2008. Web. 28 Nov. 2008. <http://www.funbrain.com/funbrain/who/index.html>.

Appendix A

Let's Collaborate!

1. At the end of our unit, we would like for our students to be able to

_____

_____

_____

_____

2. What curriculum standards will we include?

Content

_____

_____

_____

_____

_____

_____

_____

_____

Information Literacy

_____

_____

_____

_____

_____

_____

_____

_____

Technology

_____

_____

_____

_____

_____

_____

_____

_____

3. How will we assess that students have met these standards?

_____

_____

_____

_____

_____

Okay, now let's plan the lessons!

Let's meet again on _____ .
We will bring _____
_____ .

Appendix B

LET'S PLAN OUR LESSONS

Date: _____

What to bring to the meeting:

- Your personal planning calendar

- Your curriculum documents (use the standards that your school system requires)

  - National standards

  - State standards

  - Local standards

- Lesson plans you have used previously (use these as building blocks for collaboration)

  - Artifacts

  - Exemplary work

- Resources that you would like to use with this unit

  - Books

  - Online databases that your school system has purchased

  - Web sites

  - Other reference materials

  - Manipulatives

THINK ABOUT YOUR COLLABORATIVE UNIT

Think about whether this will be a collaborative unit or a single lesson. How will this unit/ lesson look and be implemented whether taught in the classroom, library media center, or by co-teaching in either location:

- What objectives will we use?
  - Students should be able to use:
    - Bloom's Taxonomy
      - http://www.teachers.ash.org.au/researchskills/dalton.htm
      - http://nerds.unl.edu/pages/preser/sec/articles/blooms.html
- What lessons have I used in the past that may be useful?
  - Lesson ideas
    - _____
    - _____

- How does this lesson require that our students perform an authentic task?
  - Real-life task
    - _____
    - _____

- Could the final product be changed to improve student learning?
  - Final product ideas
    - _____
    - _____

- How can we implement the use of technology into this lesson?
  - Internet
    - _____
  - Online databases
    - _____
  - Hardware
    - _____

- Software

  - _____

- Think about current concerns for student achievement in your classroom.

  - Identify concerns

    - Individual Educational Plan (IEP)

    - Student behaviors

    - _____

  - How will these concerns be addressed?

    - _____

- Who will teach the objectives?

  - Library media specialist

    - _____

  - Classroom teacher

    - _____

  - Both

    - _____

  - Other teacher

    - _____

- Where will the learning occur?

  - Classroom

  - Library media center

  - Computer lab

  - Other

- Who will create the materials?

  - New materials

    - _____

  - Adapted materials

    - _____

- We will need to obtain

    - _____

    - _____

- Who will collect and grade students' work?

    - Library media specialist

    - Classroom teacher

    - Both

        - _____

        - _____

    - Other

- Does this lesson/unit remind us of another lesson/unit on which we could collaborate?

    - _____

LESSON PLAN TEMPLATE

Unit Name:

Grade Level:

Lesson Name:

Standards:

Objectives:

Time Required:

Materials List:

Materials We Need To Obtain:

Lesson Procedures:

- Engagement: (The engagement should grab your students' attention and set the stage for what is to follow.)

- Activity: (Explain to students what they will do.)

- Transition: (Give students time to complete a task, or transition them to another are—more than one transition may be required.)

- Activity: (Explain to students what they will continue to do.)

- Closure: (Verify that your students have learned the objectives selected for this lesson.)

- Assessment: (Visual, performance based, or ongoing.)

OUR REFLECTION OF THIS UNIT

Unit Name:

Teachers Involved with this Unit:

Grade Level:

Lesson Names:

What were the strengths of this unit?

What could be improved next time?

- Timing of lessons

- Student considerations

- Collaborative changes

- Other teachers that could be involved

- Changing the final product

- Adding, removing, or changing lessons

- Adding, removing, or changing technology integration

Were additional resources or materials needed? If so, what was needed and why?

Another collaborative idea may be:

Index

About the Authors

DANIELLE N. DUPUIS began her career with libraries as an information specialist for Howard County Library in 2001. After graduating in 2005 from the College of Library and Information Studies program at University of Maryland with her Master of Library Science degree, she was hired as a library media specialist for Howard County Public Schools. Danielle became a Google Certified Teacher in 2009 and received a Master's Certificate from Johns Hopkins University in Instructional Technology for Web-based Professional Development in 2010. Her first book, written with colleague and friend Annette C. H. Nelson, was *The Adventures of Super3: A Teacher's Guide to Information Literacy for Grades K-2,* published in July 2010. Danielle continues to educate students attending Howard County Public Schools.

LORI M. CARTER began her career in education in 1996 as a classroom teacher after graduating from Bowie State University, Bowie, Maryland. In 2000 Lori became an elementary library media specialist after graduating from the College of Library and Information Studies program at the University of Maryland with her Master of Library Science degree. In 2002 she became Nationally Board Certified in Library Media/Early Childhood through Young Adult. Lori holds Master's Certificates in both Administration (2003; McDaniel College in Westminster, MD) and Leadership in Technology Integration (2008; Johns Hopkins University, Baltimore, MD). Currently, Lori is an instructional technology teacher for Howard County Public Schools and serves as the professional development liaison at Forest Ridge Elementary School in Laurel, Maryland. In addition, Lori teaches as an online adjunct faculty member for the Master's of Arts in Teaching Program at National University, La Jolla, California. She lives in Crofton, Maryland, with her husband, Rick, and their family.

Danielle and Lori met at curriculum writing during the summer of 2006. Both discovered that their similar views of education in the library media field could be attributed to the education they received from the College of Library and Information Studies program at University of Maryland. Sharing similar views and beliefs in education gave them the foundation necessary to write the Destination Collaboration books together. However, the drive, determination, passion, and persistence shared between the two was what held them together through edit after edit and rewrite after rewrite during a three-year period of mostly collaboration with a fair amount of coordination and cooperation.